Fast Starters, Soups and Salads

Fast Starters, Soups and Salads

by

Mary Berry

PIATKUS

My grateful thanks to Clare Blunt for her meticulous help in developing and testing these recipes, and for all her support during the eight years we have worked together.

First published in 1983 by
Judy Piatkus (Publishers) Limited of Loughton, Essex

British Library Cataloguing in Publication Data

Berry, Mary
    Fast starters, soups + salads.
    1. Cookery (Appetizers)
    I. Title
    641.8′12   TX740

    ISBN 0-86188-231-8

Typeset by Phoenix Photosetting, Chatham, Kent

Printed in Great Britain by
The Garden City Press Limited,
Letchworth, Hertfordshire SG6 1JS

Contents

Illustrations

INTRODUCTION

The first course, affectionately called the starter, is a vital part of the meal and it is composed of such delicious ingredients that it could well be a feast in its own right. There is home-made soup in all its variety, there are creamy meat and fish pâtés, fresh vegetables, asparagus in butter, and prawns, mushrooms, shrimps . . . the list goes on. Who *does* need anything more?

But you can have the best of both worlds. The first course at dinner must of necessity be limited in quantity, otherwise it will spoil the effect of what follows. Its function is to whet the appetite, to leave the diner in a state of eager anticipation of the delights to come. On the other hand there is no possible reason why you should not make the same starter dishes, using the same ingredients, in larger quantities, to serve for lunch or supper. When preparing dinner it is often easy enough to make more than you will need of the starter and to freeze it for use later.

We are all in a hurry these days and feeding the family or cooking for guests is only a part of our lives. The beauty of the recipes in this book is that they are fast and simple to make. Average preparation time is about ten minutes and cooking, where necessary, takes less than an hour, while there are pâtés that can be made in five minutes flat.

Much of the preparation can often be done in advance, to leave the cook free to concentrate on other duties – whether these duties are basting the joint in the oven, or seeing that the children are in bed before the guests arrive.

There is more to dinner than the cooking and serving of three or more courses. Planning a balanced menu comes into it too. How you start the meal is as important as all first impressions are, and the first course should contrast with as well as complement what comes next. You will not of course serve a substantial soup before a rich beef casserole – particularly not at the height of summer – nor will you offer your guests chilled grapefruit before cold meats on a winter night. Adjust your catering to the time of year.

Serve fresh food when you can and choose the best quality you can

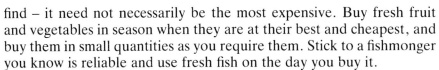

find – it need not necessarily be the most expensive. Buy fresh fruit and vegetables in season when they are at their best and cheapest, and buy them in small quantities as you require them. Stick to a fishmonger you know is reliable and use fresh fish on the day you buy it.

Fresh ingredients are the ideal to aim at, but modern methods of freezing, packaging and preserving foodstuffs have made life easier for the cook. Don't be afraid to take full advantage of them. Fast cooking does not imply instant food. Use packaged goods as an addition to other foods, not as a substitute. Canned condensed soups – tomato, mushroom and celery for example – are invaluable for making a quick sauce; chicken or beef stock cubes stand in for home-made stock in soups; and even instant mashed potato makes a good pie topping, sprinkled with cheese perhaps and browned under the grill, and it can also be used to thicken soups.

These convenience foods are just a part of a dish and a help in cutting corners. The good cook adds her individual touches with seasoning, herbs and garnishes.

The freezer is a real friend to the fast cook. Pâtés and terrines, for instance, can be made in advance and frozen for later use. A batch of frozen pastry can be thawed and brought quickly into service. Pastry cases can be instantly available. Freeze canned tomato purée in the ice cube tray then transfer to a polythene bag and remove just the quantity you want when you need it. A fast soup becomes considerably slower if you have to stop and make croûtons for it as you go along, so make a good supply of them and keep them frozen. Freeze breadcrumbs too, and grated cheese, Cheddar or Parmesan, ready for immediate use. Keep a stock of frozen cream. You can now buy both whipping and double in bags; it is in pieces, so you can thaw just the amount you need.

A well-stocked larder is essential. With a good supply of foodstuffs on the shelves there is no need to fear unexpected guests, no reason to panic if you come home late to face a hungry family. Among basics for the store cupboard are: cans of condensed soups, including consommé; cans of tomatoes, pimentos, sweetcorn, asparagus tips, artichoke hearts; canned fish such as tuna (one of the most useful), crab, salmon, sardines, and anchovies; olives. Among the dry basics you will need rice, pasta of different kinds, flour, beans, lentils; mustard, spices, including curry powder and paprika; your favourite herbs. Keep Worcestershire sauce, tomato sauce, anchovy essence, Long Life milk (good for soups and sauces), pickles and chutneys.

Jars of lump-fish roe are useful. You can make a quick omelette and garnish it with sour cream and spoonfuls of roe, red and black, and so turn a faithful standby into a festive dish.

Keep a stock of vacuum-packed meats from the delicatessen – ham, liver sausage, garlic sausage. These are best stored in the fridge and need no preparation. Remember that lemons and citrus fruits will keep for ages in a polythene bag in the fridge. And do keep a good supply of eggs and cheese.

These are all basic essentials. You will certainly find yourself adding to them according to your personal taste.

When there is a question of speed in the kitchen the modern cook has an enormous advantage over her predecessors. Electrical equipment available today has cut food preparation time down to a minimum. The blender or liquidiser prepares purées and soups with a minimum of effort, while the more versatile food processor mixes, chops, slices, sieves, shreds and purées in literally seconds. If you make a lot of pâtés and soups it is an almost essential investment.

Soups

Soup is a universally popular first course and it can just as well be the main part of lunch or supper, in which case it will be a substantial and nourishing one, probably followed by cheese or salad, or pâté with crusty bread. As a dinner starter, suit it to the courses that follow, make it light and well flavoured, not to spoil the appetite. Make it decorative to look at, garnished with a swirl of cream, with chopped parsley or chives, or hand a basket of cheese straws with it.

Make your own stock and freeze it. I make mine rather concentrated as it takes up less space in the freezer. Failing that, use stock cubes or canned condensed soup suitably dressed up.

Meat Starters

Use a blender or food processor to make your own pâtés, which may be based on either meat or fish. Pâté makes the first course simplicity itself. Just thaw it or bring to room temperature, cut it in slices and serve with hot toast or crusty bread and butter. For a light lunch serve it after a good vegetable soup. Use your vacuum-packed cooked meats with a variety of different ingredients to make deliciously different – and easy – first courses.

Fish Starters

Fish is quickly cooked and for a first course you do not need a great deal, so you may feel like spending on an expensive variety. On the other hand, smoked salmon pieces from the delicatessen are more economical than slices and, with a little ingenuity, every bit as good. Fill a bought flan case with a mixture of smoked salmon trimmings, eggs and cream and put it in the oven for about half an hour, and what could be simpler? A small quantity of smoked fish can be used to make pâtés and creams which will introduce your meal superbly.

There are more ways of serving prawns than the ubiquitous prawn cocktail, and even that can be given a different flavour with the addition of a little horseradish cream. Try combining prawns with melon, or in prawn cocottes for a good lunch or supper dish. When using frozen prawns, let them thaw slowly to preserve their flavour.

For a change, serve scallops, cockles or mussels, and don't overlook whitebait, one of the best fish starters of all.

Vegetable Starters

Vegetables make some of the fastest and least expensive first courses. Fresh ones are always good and they are best served simply. Globe artichokes in butter are quick and easy. So are stuffed tomatoes, which need no cooking. If you can get them, use the Dutch beefsteak tomatoes; they are large and impressive and have an excellent flavour. Don't stop at tomatoes. Make stuffings for peppers, courgettes, aubergines and mushrooms too. Or serve mushrooms raw with a French dressing – use the tiny white button ones for this. Asparagus with melted butter is everyone's idea of a treat and it need not be expensive if you buy sprue, the long thin stalks which are green all the way down, so that you can eat almost the whole of them.

For a change, offer your guests *crudités* either with pre-dinner drinks or as the first course. These are simply small pieces of raw vegetables – cauliflower, carrots, onion, cucumber, peppers, radishes – served with a bowl of sauce to dip them in. Arrange the raw vegetables attractively, using their contrasting colours to advantage, and provide perhaps three bowls of different dips – there is a particularly good curry flavoured one – and let your guests help themselves.

We all know cauliflower au gratin, but there is no reason to stop at cauliflower. Most vegetables can be served *au gratin*, an excellent way of using up any that are left over. Save time by cooking more vegetables than you need for dinner and using the remainder for lunch next day.

Fruit Starters

If you are serving a rich or substantial main dish, fruit is the ideal first course. It is light, refreshing and appetising and very welcome on a warm summer evening. Grapefruit, avocado and melon need no introduction, but try them in different combinations and with other fruit. Aim at lightness and freshness.

Eggs, Bread and Cheese Starters

There is a lot more to the sandwich than slices of cheese or ham between slices of bread. A good sandwich can be a work of art, a delicious bite to start a meal, or a meal in itself. The Scandinavians are masters of the art of the open sandwich – buttered rye bread, covered according to taste with a huge selection of savoury and sweet ingredients, arranged with skill and imagination. The secret of quick assembly here is to have all your materials to hand before you begin.

An alternative to the sandwich is the quiche. Fill the flan case with the classic egg and cheese mixture or ring the changes with bacon, onion, leeks, tuna, salmon. Make a large quiche and cut it in wedges for a main dish or make tiny individual quiches for a first course or to hand round with drinks.

Eggs and cheese are a blessing to the fast cook, the reliable standbys that go together in innumerable dishes, that combine so well with other foods, that are easy to store and to use and that are always ready to come to the rescue when a meal is wanted in a hurry.

Put them together in individual cheese soufflés that can be made in advance and frozen until needed. Make stuffed hard-boiled eggs, or egg mousse, or Chinese omelettes. They all start a meal in style, or they can be served for a summer lunch or a later supper.

Salads

A salad may be a course in its own right or it may complement another dish. Preceded by home-made soup it is a good simple lunch; served in individual dishes with an interesting dressing it is a pleasant prelude to dinner. Salads are fast to make, a matter of assembling rather than cooking. The secret is variety and crispness. If you have really fresh ingredients you can combine them as your imagination suggests, contrasting colours and textures. A good salad must *look* good.

You can buy excellent mayonnaise and French dressing, but do be encouraged to make your own and keep them in the fridge. Experiment with new flavours. Add lemon juice, curry powder, mustard or herbs. Use fresh herbs if you can, they add nothing to the cost but a lot to the flavour. Try growing your own in the garden, or in a window-box, or even in pots on the kitchen windowsill.

Sauces and Garnishes

The successful cook pays attention to details. The garnish often makes the dish. The croûtons for the soup, the mayonnaise and dressing for the salad, the tartare sauce for the fish are all easily prepared in advance. Different flavourings can be added to a basic sauce – tomato, garlic, herbs as required. Garlic bread, cheese straws or cheese fingers and melba toast are simple but all-important additions to many a home-made soup.

All keen cooks have their favourite dishes, tried and tested, and most of them are constantly adding to their collection. The recipes that follow are designed for all tastes and all occasions. They are for family meals, sophisticated dinner parties, light lunches, for impromptu suppers round the fire, summer evenings in the garden. Most of all, they are for *you*.

SOUPS

Soup is versatile. It may be the first course, or it may be the main part of the meal. If it is the introduction to dinner you will of course keep it light and well flavoured to tempt the taste buds. In summer it may even be cold. If it is a prelude to perhaps pâté and crusty bread, or to a crips salad or a light egg dish, you will make it more substantial, and you will probably make more than you need and use the rest for lunch next day.

Soup *can* be quickly made. There is a seven-minute tomato one from ingredients in most store cupboards.

The wise cook makes chicken or beef stock in quantity and freezes it to use when needed. If you are out of home-made stock you can use chicken or beef stock cubes, or canned consommé. Canned condensed soups are invaluable when you are in a hurry, but remember that they are only the *basis* of the dish, and make your own additions – chopped chicken, mushroom stalks, prawns. Instant potato from a packet is useful too for thickening.

Soups should be good to look at as well as to eat. Decorate them attractively and imaginatively. Chopped chives, sprigs of watercress, a swirl of cream, or asparagus tips, for instance, take no time to prepare and make a world of difference to the appearance. Serve too, with interesting garnishes (see page 187).

A blender or food processor cuts down preparation time enormously, and for some soup recipes it is a must.

Asparagus Soup

A quick cheat soup.

Preparation time about 10 minutes
Cooking time about 10 minutes

1 oz (25 g) butter
1 oz (25 g) flour
½ pint (300 ml) chicken stock
½ pint (300 ml) milk
salt
freshly ground black pepper
pinch of sugar
12-oz (340-g) can asparagus tips
a few drops green colouring

Melt the butter in a saucepan, stir in the flour and cook for a minute. Blend in the stock and milk and bring to the boil, stirring, until the sauce has thickened. Add seasoning and sugar.

Drain the liquor from the can of asparagus and add to the pan. Cut off a few asparagus tips for garnish and add the rest to the soup, then cover and simmer for 10 minutes.

Purée the soup in a processor or blender and then return to the saucepan and reheat, adding a few drops of green colouring. Taste and check seasoning and if the soup seems a little thick add some extra milk.

Pour into bowls and garnish with the reserved asparagus tips.

Serves 4 small portions

Seven-Minute Tomato Soup

Make in 7 minutes flat from ingredients that are usually in the house.

Preparation time about 7 minutes
Cooking time about 7 minutes

1 oz (25 g) butter
1 small onion, finely chopped
1 oz (25 g) flour
½ pint (300 ml) water
2½-oz (62-g) can tomato purée
½ pint (300 ml) milk
1 teaspoon caster sugar
salt
freshly ground black pepper
grated Parmesan cheese
chopped parsley

Melt the butter in a saucepan, add the onion and fry gently for about 5 minutes, or until soft but not coloured. Stir in the flour and cook for a minute, without colouring.

Draw the pan off the heat and gradually add the water and tomato purée. Stir until smooth and then return to the heat and bring to the boil, stiring until thickened. Add the milk, sugar and seasoning, stir until well blended and then simmer gently for 7 minutes.

Taste and check seasoning. Pour into bowls, sprinkle with cheese and parsley, and serve at once.

Serves 2 to 3

Carrot Soup

On special occasions it is very nice to add swirls of yogurt or cream to the soup just before serving and garnish with chopped parsley. *(Illustrated on the jacket.)*

Preparation time about 10 minutes
Cooking time about 15 minutes

  1 oz (25 g) butter
  1 small onion, chopped
  1 lb (450 g) carrots, sliced
  1½ pints (900 ml) chicken stock
  1 bayleaf
  salt and pepper

Melt the butter in a saucepan, add the onion and carrots, cover the saucepan and cook the vegetables gently for 5 to 10 minutes, without colouring.

Pour on the stock, add the bayleaf and seasoning, and bring the soup to the boil stirring. Cover and simmer for 15 minutes or until the vegetables are tender.

Remove the bayleaf and then sieve or purée the soup in a blender or processor. Rinse out the saucepan and return the soup to it. Bring to the boil, taste and check the seasoning, pour into a tureen and serve very hot.

Serves 4

Orange Soup

Orange and carrots make a delicious combination. Serve this soup for a special meal.

Preparation time about 5 minutes
Cooking time about 5 minutes

1 lb, 2-oz (524-g) can carrots, drained
1 pint (600 ml) chicken stock
6-oz (175-g) can frozen concentrated orange juice, just thawed
salt and pepper

Purée the carrots in a blender or processor and put in a saucepan with the stock and orange juice. Bring to the boil, stirring.

Simmer gently for 5 minutes, taste and check seasoning and serve very hot. If liked a swirl of cream may be stirred into each portion before serving.

Serves 4

Leek and Celery Soup

A simple vegetable soup, full of flavour and chunky. Serve as a first course followed perhaps by crusty bread and pâté.

Preparation time about 10 minutes
Cooking time about 30 minutes

 2 oz (50 g) butter
 1 lb (450 g) leeks, finely sliced
 1 head celery, finely sliced
 1¾ pints (1 litre) chicken stock
 salt
 freshly ground black pepper
 ¼ pint (150 ml) single cream

Melt the butter in a large saucepan, add the leeks and celery and fry slowly for 10 minutes to soften the vegetables without colouring.

Add the stock with salt and pepper (the amount will depend on the seasoning in the stock), and bring to the boil, stirring. Cover the saucepan, reduce the heat and simmer for 30 minutes or until the vegetables are quite tender.

Taste and check seasoning and then just before serving stir in the cream.

Serves 4 to 6

Devon Vegetable Soup

Make this soup only if you have bacon or ham stock on hand, otherwise it really isn't a fast soup.

Preparation time about 2 minutes
Cooking time about 25 minutes

    1 lb (450 g) mixed root vegetables, finely diced
    2 pints (a good litre) ham or bacon stock
    1 bayleaf
    a good pinch mixed dried herbs
    salt and pepper
    4 oz (100 g) finely diced cooked ham or bacon
    ¼ pint (150 ml) single cream

Put the vegetables, stock, bayleaf, herbs and seasoning in a saucepan, and bring to the boil. Cover the pan and simmer for about 25 minutes or until the vegetables are tender.

Taste and check seasoning, remove bayleaf, and add the diced ham or bacon. Stir in the cream and reheat the soup but do not boil.

Serve at once.

Serves 4 to 6

Golden Vegetable Soup

A colourful soup, ideal for serving on a chilly evening before cheese or pâté.

Preparation time about 15 minutes
Cooking time about 30 minutes

1 lb (450 g) old potatoes
1 lb (450 g) carrots
2 leeks, sliced
2 oz (50 g) butter
2 pints (a good litre) chicken stock (or ham stock if available)
salt and pepper
1/4 pint (150 ml) milk

Coarsely grate the potatoes and carrots and mix with the leeks. Melt the butter in a large roomy saucepan and add the vegetables. Cover the pan and cook without colouring, stirring occasionally, for 10 minutes.

Add the stock to the saucepan with salt and pepper (about 2 teaspoons of salt, probably, but this will depend on the seasoning in the stock). Cover the saucepan and simmer for 30 minutes or until the vegetables are tender.

Stir the milk into the soup, taste and check seasoning, and serve hot.

Serves 5 to 6

Green Watercress Soup

Use the very best sprigs of watercress in salad or for garnishing the main course, then put the remainder including the stalks in the soup. Don't tackle this soup unless you have an electric blender or processor. Packet potato is perfect for this recipe, but avoid keeping the soup hot for long as the colour and flavour will deteriorate.

Preparation time about 15 minutes
Cooking time about 10 minutes

2 bunches watercress
1 oz (25 g) butter
1 medium onion, chopped
1½ pints (900 ml) stock
salt and freshly ground black pepper
4.62-oz (131-g) packet instant mashed potato
¾ pint (450 ml) milk

Thoroughly wash both bunches of watercress and put a few small sprigs on one side for garnish. Cut the remainder in short lengths with scissors.

Melt the butter in a large saucepan over a low heat, add the onion and fry gently for 10 minutes until soft but not coloured. Add the watercress, stock and seasoning and bring to the boil and simmer for 5 minutes.

Purée the soup in a processor or blender in 3 or 4 batches and then return to the rinsed saucepan. Stir in the contents of the packet of instant mashed potato and bring to the boil. Stir in the milk, heat through and then taste and check seasoning.

Turn into a tureen and float the sprigs of watercress on top.

Serves 4 to 6

French Onion Soup

Such a glorious soup to have when it is cold and there is little else to follow – perfect for Sunday night around the fire.

Preparation time about 12 minutes
Cooking time about 20 minutes

> *2 oz (50 g) dripping*
> *1 lb (450 g) onions, finely chopped*
> *2 level teaspoons sugar*
> *1 oz (25 g) flour*
> *2 pints (a good litre) beef stock*
> *salt and pepper*
> *4 slices French bread*
> *2 oz (50 g) Gruyère cheese, grated*

Melt the dripping in a saucepan, add the onions and sugar and fry gently, stirring occasionally, until golden brown. Be careful not to let them burn otherwise the soup will taste bitter. This will take about 10 minutes.

Stir in the flour and cook for a minute, then add the stock and bring to the boil, stirring. Add salt and pepper, cover the saucepan and simmer for 20 minutes. Taste and check seasoning.

Toast the French bread on one side, then sprinkle the cheese on the untoasted side and put under the grill to melt.

Place a slice of bread in each soup bowl and then pour over the soup. Serve at once.

Serves 4

Creamed Stilton and Onion Soup

This soup is made from a popular combination, and is excellent served with French bread. *(See picture facing page 32.)*

Preparation time about 10 minutes
Cooking time about 15 minutes

2 oz (50 g) butter
12 oz (350 g) onions, chopped
2 oz (50 g) flour
¾ pint (450 ml) chicken stock
¾ pint (450 ml) milk
6 oz (175 g) Stilton cheese, roughly chopped
1 tablespoon Worcestershire sauce
salt
freshly ground black pepper
chopped chives or parsley to garnish

Heat the butter in a large saucepan, add the onion and fry gently for about 5 minutes. Stir in the flour and cook for a minute. Gradually add the stock and milk, stirring continuously, and bring to the boil. Reduce the heat and then add the Stilton, Worcestershire sauce and seasoning. Cover the pan and simmer for 15 minutes.

Purée in a blender or processor in 2 or 3 batches. Rinse out the saucepan, return the soup to it and reheat. Taste and check seasoning.

Serve sprinkled with chopped chives or parsley.

Serves 4 to 6

Kidney and Onion Soup

An inexpensive filling sort of winter soup. I always make more than I need as it is welcome for lunch next day.

Preparation time about 10 minutes
Cooking time about 20 minutes

> *8 oz (225 g) ox kidney*
> *1 oz (25 g) dripping*
> *1 large onion, chopped*
> *2 pints (a good litre) beef stock*
> *2 teaspoons tomato purée*
> *1 bayleaf*
> *good pinch mixed herbs*
> *salt and pepper*
> *1 rounded tablespoon cornflour*
> *2 tablespoons sherry*

Remove any core from the kidney and cut into small pieces.

Melt the dripping in a saucepan and add the kidney and onion and fry for 5 minutes, stirring occasionally. Add the stock, tomato purée, bayleaf, herbs and seasoning, and bring to the boil. Cover the saucepan and simmer for for about 20 minutes or until the kidney is tender.

Remove the bayleaf. Put the cornflour in the blender or processor with the sherry and run until blended, then add some of the soup and purée. Turn into a bowl and purée the remaining soup in 2 or 3 batches.

Return the soup to the saucepan and bring to the boil, stirring, and then taste and check seasoning. Turn into a tureen and serve piping hot.

Serves 4 to 6

Creamy Mushroom Soup

Mushroom stalks are often sold in greengrocers at a few pence a quarter and are ideal for this soup.

Preparation time about 15 minutes
Cooking time about 5 minutes

2 oz (50 g) butter
1 small onion, chopped
8 oz (225 g) mushroom stalks, chopped
2 oz (50 g) flour
1¼ pints (750 ml) chicken stock
salt
freshly ground black pepper
½ pint (300 ml) milk

Melt the butter in a saucepan, add the onion and cook gently for 5 minutes, then add the mushrooms and continue cooking for a further 5 minutes.

Sprinkle in the flour and cook for a minute, then blend in the stock, stirring well. Bring the soup to the boil, stirring continuously until thickened. Add salt and pepper and simmer gently for 5 minutes.

Purée the soup in a processor or blender in 2 or 3 batches and then return to the saucepan with the milk and bring to the boil, stirring. Taste and check seasoning and if the soup seems a little thick add some extra milk.

Turn into a tureen and serve piping hot.

Serves 4

Cream of Spinach Soup

This is best when made with good stock, ideally chicken.

Preparation time about 15 minutes
Cooking time about 15 minutes

2 oz (50 g) butter
2 onions, chopped
2 oz (50 g) flour
1½ pints (900 ml) chicken stock
10.6-oz (300-g) packet spinach, frozen
good pinch nutmeg
salt
freshly ground black pepper
¼ pint (150 ml) single cream

Melt the butter in a saucepan, add the onion and cook gently for 10 minutes, so that the onion is tender but not brown. Stir in the flour and cook for a minute. Add the stock and bring to the boil, stirring until thickened. Add the block of spinach, nutmeg, salt and pepper, cover the pan and simmer for about 15 minutes, when the spinach will have cooked.

Purée the soup in a processor or blender in 2 or 3 batches. Rinse out the saucepan and return the soup to it.

Reheat the soup, taste and check seasoning and, when ready to serve, stir in the cream and serve at once, in a hot tureen.

Serves 4

Bacon and Spinach Soup

A delicious warming soup, very good on a cold day. *(See picture facing page 32.)*

Preparation time about 15 minutes
Cooking time about 20 minutes

2 oz (50 g) butter
1 large onion, chopped
6 oz (175 g) streaky bacon, chopped
1 lb (450 g) frozen spinach
1 oz (25 g) flour
³⁄₄ pint (450 ml) milk
³⁄₄ pint (450 ml) chicken stock
1 tablespoon Worcestershire sauce
salt
freshly ground black pepper
¹⁄₄ pint (150 ml) single cream

Heat the butter in a large saucepan, add the onion and bacon and fry gently for about 5 minutes until soft. Add the spinach, then cover the pan and cook gently for 10 minutes.

Stir the flour into the spinach and cook for a minute. Gradually add the milk and stock, stirring constantly. Add the Worcestershire sauce and seasoning, bring to the boil, cover and simmer for 20 minutes.

Purée the soup in a blender or processor. Rinse out the saucepan, return the soup to it and bring to the boil. Taste and check seasoning. Remove the pan from the heat and stir in all but a tablespoon of the cream.

Turn into a serving dish or tureen and swirl the remaining cream on top.

Serves 6

Cream of Lettuce Soup

Bolted lettuces from the garden are always a problem, but this soup uses them up very well.

Preparation time about 15 minutes
Cooking time about 10 minutes

1½ oz (40 g) butter
small bunch chives
1 lettuce, shredded
1 onion, roughly chopped
1 potato, roughly chopped
1 oz (25 g) flour
¾ pint (450 ml) chicken stock
¾ pint (450 ml) milk
a good pinch nutmeg
salt and black pepper
5 tablespoons single cream

Melt the butter in a large saucepan, add the chives and vegetables, cover and cook over a gentle heat for 10 minutes, without colouring.

Sprinkle in the flour, stir well, and then add the stock and milk with nutmeg and seasoning, and bring to the boil, stirring. Simmer the soup for 10 minutes or until the vegetables are tender.

Purée the soup in a processor or blender, in 2 or 3 batches. Rinse out the saucepan and return the soup to it. Reheat until very hot and taste and check seasoning. Pour into bowls and swirl a little cream on top of each bowl.

Serves 4

Cream of Parsnip Soup

A superb soup, always very popular in our house, quite good enough for a dinner or supper party.

Preparation time about 15 minutes
Cooking time about 25 minutes

> 3 oz (75 g) butter
> 1 onion, chopped
> 1 lb (450 g) parsnip, cubed
> 1 oz (25 g) flour
> 1 rounded teaspoon curry powder
> 2 pints (a good litre) beef stock
> salt and pepper
> 1/4 pint (150 ml) single cream
> chopped parsley

Melt the butter in a large saucepan, add the onion and parsnip, and fry gently for 10 minutes. Stir in the flour and curry powder and cook for a minute, then add the stock and seasoning and bring to the boil, stirring. Cover the saucepan and simmer gently for 25 minutes or until the parsnip is tender.

Purée the soup in a blender or processor in 2 or 3 batches. Rinse out the saucepan and return the soup to it. Reheat and taste and check seasoning.

When ready to serve, remove from the heat and stir in the cream. Pour into a tureen and sprinkle with chopped parsley.

Serves 6

Curry Soup

An unusual soup, well worth making for a change, and is particularly good if served with fried poppadums instead of rolls or bread.

Preparation time about 20 minutes
Cooking time about 15 minutes

2 tablespoons desiccated coconut
¼ pint (150 ml) boiling water
1 oz (25 g) butter
1 level tablespoon curry powder
1 onion, finely chopped
1 oz (25 g) flour
1½ pints (900 ml) chicken stock
1½ lb (675 g) cooking apples, peeled, cored and roughly chopped
juice of half a lemon
1 tablespoon redcurrant jelly
salt and pepper
chopped parsley

Put the coconut in a bowl, pour on boiling water and infuse for 20 minutes.

Meanwhile melt the butter in a saucepan, add the curry powder and onion, cover and cook gently, stirring occasionally, for 10 minutes. Stir in the flour and cook for a minute, then add the stock and bring to the boil, stirring until thickened.

Strain the liquor from the coconut and add to the soup (discarding the coconut). Add the apples, lemon juice, redcurrant jelly and seasoning. Cover the pan and simmer for 15 minutes or until the apples are tender.

Purée the soup in a processor or blender in 2 or 3 batches. Rinse out the saucepan, return the soup to it and bring to the boil. Taste and check seasoning, adding a little extra stock if the soup is too thick. Pour into a tureen and sprinkle with parsley.

Serves 6

Special Chestnut Soup

You do have to think ahead for this recipe – you have to soak the chestnuts overnight – but it is simple to make. Dried chestnuts are available from health food shops and good delicatessens.

Preparation time about 15 minutes
Cooking time about 45 minutes

6 oz (175 g) dried chestnuts
2 oz (50 g) butter
2 onions, chopped
2 pints (a good litre) chicken stock
salt and freshly ground black pepper
3 to 4 tablespoons sherry
a little cream (optional)

Place the chestnuts in a bowl, cover with cold water and leave to soak overnight. Next day peel off any dark skin, place in a saucepan, cover with cold water and bring to the boil. Simmer gently for 5 minutes, then drain.

Melt the butter in a saucepan, add the onion and chestnuts and fry gently for 5 minutes, until the onions are a pale golden brown. Add the stock and seasoning and bring to the boil. Cover the pan and simmer for 45 minutes or until the chestnuts are soft and floury.

Purée in a processor or blender in 3 or 4 batches, then return to the pan and bring to the boil. Stir in the sherry and taste and check seasoning.

Serve piping hot in a tureen, and swirl a little cream through the soup just before serving, if you like.

Serves 4

Lentil Soup

I like to serve this soup sprinkled with crispy pieces of fried bacon. Remember that the lentils need to be soaked overnight.

Preparation time about 15 minutes
Cooking time about 45 minutes

4 oz (100 g) red lentils
1½ oz (40 g) butter
1 large onion, sliced
1 large carrot, sliced
2 sticks celery, sliced
1½ pints (900 ml) stock or water
1 bayleaf
salt
1 level teaspoon paprika
good pinch cayenne pepper

Place the lentils in a bowl, cover with cold water and leave to stand overnight. Next day drain thoroughly.

Melt the butter in a saucepan, add the vegetables and cook gently for 10 minutes, stirring occasionally. Add the remaining ingredients, including the lentils, and bring the soup to the boil. Cover and simmer gently for about 45 minutes or until the lentils are tender. Remove the bayleaf and then purée the soup in a processor or blender.

Rinse out the saucepan and return the soup to it, bring to the boil, taste and check seasoning and serve very hot.

Serve 5 to 6

Right: Bacon and Spinach Soup (page 27), Mediterranean Fish Soup (page 38), and Creamed Stilton and Onion Soup (page 23).

Turkey Cranberry Soup

This is a good soup to make from left-over roast turkey. *(See picture opposite.)*

Preparation time about 45 minutes
Cooking time about 10 minutes

> *1 turkey carcass*
> *2 pints (a good litre) water*
> *2 oz (50 g) turkey dripping or butter*
> *1 onion, chopped*
> *2 oz (50 g) plain flour*
> *6 to 8 oz (175 to 225 g) cooked left-over turkey, finely diced*
> *1 tablespoon mustard*
> *salt*
> *freshly ground black pepper*
> *4 tablespoons cranberry sauce*

Put the turkey carcass in a saucepan with the water. Bring to the boil and simmer for 35 minutes. Drain off the stock and discard the bones.

Melt the dripping or butter in a large saucepan and fry the onion for about 10 minutes until soft but not brown. Stir in the flour and cook gently until golden brown. Add the stock and bring to the boil, stirring until smooth. Add the turkey and mustard and season well. Simmer for 10 minutes.

Purée the soup in a blender or processor in 2 or 3 batches. Rinse out the saucepan and return the soup to it. Reheat, then taste and adjust seasoning. Stir in the cranberry sauce just before serving.

Serves 4 to 6

Left: Turkey Cranberry Soup (above).

Parkgate Shrimp Soup

I first made this soup from shrimps bought from Parkgate in the Wirral where they are all hand-packed in the local cottages. Now I make the soup using Young's potted shrimps.

Preparation time about 10 minutes
Cooking time about 5 minutes

1½ oz (40 g) butter
1½ oz (40 g) flour
1½ pints (900 ml) milk
2 teaspoons anchovy essence
salt
freshly ground black pepper
2 × 1.76-oz (50-g) cartons potted shrimps
2 teaspoons tomato purée
1 tablespoon chopped parsley

Melt the butter in a saucepan, stir in the flour and cook for a minute. Add the milk and anchovy essence and bring to the boil, stirring.

Season and add the potted shrimps with the tomato purée, stirring well so that the purée colours the soup a delicate pink. Simmer gently for 5 minutes, stirring occasionally so that the butter from the shrimps melts and flavours the soup.

Taste and check seasoning, then pour into a tureen and serve very hot, sprinkled with chopped parsley.

Serves 4 to 6

Fast Celery and Prawn Bisque

This is a thick, warming soup, ideal for a winter dinner party as the prawns give it a special lift.

Preparation time about 10 minutes
Cooking time about 25 minutes

   2 oz (50 g) butter
   1 onion, sliced
   8 oz (225 g) potatoes, peeled and diced
   1 lb, 2½-oz (524-g) can celery hearts
   1¼ pints (750 ml) milk
   1 level teaspoon paprika
   salt and pepper
   4 oz (100 g) frozen prawns, thawed

Melt the butter in a saucepan, add the onion and potato and cook gently for 5 minutes, so that they soften but not brown. Stir in the contents of the can of celery with the milk, paprika and seasoning and bring to the boil. Stir with a wooden spoon to break down the celery roughly. Reduce the heat, cover the pan and simmer for 25 minutes.

Purée the soup in 2 or 3 batches in a blender or processor, and then rinse out the saucepan and return the soup to it.

Bring to the boil and stir in the prawns, taste and check seasoning. Turn into a tureen and serve very hot.

Serves 6

Tuna Chowder

Serve before a light main course, or even bread and cheese.

Preparation time about 2 to 3 minutes
Cooking time about 7 minutes

10½-oz (298-g) can condensed tomato soup
10½-oz (298-g) can condensed cream of chicken soup
1 pint (600 ml) water
8-oz (227-g) can peas, drained
2 tablespoons dried onion flakes
7-oz (200-g) can tuna fish, drained and flaked
1 oz (25 g) quick cooking macaroni
salt and pepper

Put all the ingredients into a saucepan and bring to the boil, stirring. Cover the saucepan and simmer for 7 minutes, or until the macaroni is cooked.

Taste and check seasoning and serve at once.

Serves 4

Corn and Crab Soup

A Chinese type of soup that makes a nice change.

Preparation time about 10 minutes
Cooking time about 20 minutes

1 oz (25 g) butter
1 onion, chopped
1½ pints (900 ml) chicken stock
12-oz (340-g) can whole kernel sweetcorn, drained
salt
freshly ground black pepper
6-oz (170-g) can crab meat

Melt the butter in a saucepan, add the onion and cook gently for 5 minutes, without colouring. Add the stock, sweetcorn, salt and pepper and bring to the boil, stirring. Cover the saucepan and simmer for 20 minutes or until the corn is tender.

Purée the soup in a processor or blender in 2 or 3 batches, then return to the saucepan and bring to the boil, stirring.

Drain the crab meat, flake and remove any pieces of bone. Stir into the soup, bring to the boil, taste and check seasoning. If you find the soup a little thick, stir in some extra stock. Serve very hot.

Serves 4

Mediterranean Fish Soup

This is a very filling soup, almost a meal in itself. Serve with chunks of French bread. *(See picture facing page 32.)*

Preparation time about 10 minutes
Cooking time about 25 minutes

 2 tablespoons oil
 2 onions, sliced
 2 cloves garlic, crushed
 2 × 14-oz (397-g) cans peeled tomatoes
 2 tablespoons lemon juice
 2 tablespoons Worcestershire sauce
 1 pint (600 ml) tomato juice
 ½ pint (300 ml) water
 1 bayleaf
 salt and pepper
 12 oz (350 g) white fish, boned, skinned and cubed
 4 oz (100 g) peeled prawns

Heat the oil in a large saucepan, add the onion and garlic and fry gently for about 5 minutes until soft. Add the tomatoes, lemon juice, Worcestershire sauce, tomato juice, water, bay leaf and seasoning. Bring to the boil, then cover, reduce the heat and simmer for about 15 minutes.

Add the fish and the prawns to the saucepan and simmer for about 10 minutes.

Remove bayleaf, taste and check seasoning. Turn into a large bowl or tureen and serve.

Serves 8

Dutch Pepper Soup

Almost my favourite soup, using Dutch peppers of any colour. A must is to sieve after blending or processing to remove the pieces of pepper skin.

Preparation time about 10 minutes
Cooking time about 30 minutes

   2 tablespoons corn or vegetable oil
   2 oz (50 g) butter
   8 oz (225 g) peppers, seeded and diced
   2 onions, chopped
   1½ oz (40 g) flour
   ¾ pint (450 ml) chicken stock
   salt and pepper
   ¾ pint (450 ml) milk
   2 to 3 tablespoons single cream

Heat the oil in a saucepan, add the butter and vegetables, and cook gently for about 5 minutes, stirring occasionally. Stir in the flour and cook for a minute. Add the stock and bring to the boil, stirring until the soup has thickened. Season well, then cover the saucepan and simmer for 30 minutes or until the vegetables are soft.

Purée in a blender or processor and sieve, then rinse out the saucepan and return the soup to it with the milk. Bring to the boil, taste and check seasoning and stir in the cream.

This soup may be served either hot or very cold with extra cream.

Serves 4

Chilled Courgette Soup

Make this soup when courgettes are plentiful or you have a glut in the garden.

Preparation time about 10 minutes
Cooking time about 20 minutes

1½ oz (40 g) butter
1 lb (450 g) courgettes, sliced
15-oz (425-g) can consommé
½ bunch watercress
salt
freshly ground black pepper
¼ pint (150 ml) natural yogurt

Melt the butter in a large saucepan and add the courgettes, cover and cook gently for 5 minutes, then stir in the consommé and bring to the boil.

Trim off the thick watercress stalks and add the leaves to the pan with the seasoning. Cover and simmer for 20 minutes.

Purée the soup in a processer or blender, then put in a bowl and cover and chill thoroughly.

Taste and check seasoning and when ready to serve stir in the yogurt.

Serves 4 small portions

Chilled Summer Soup

This soup is best made with a really good home-made chicken stock, full of flavour.

Preparation time about 5 minutes
Chilling time about 1 hour

2 × 14-oz (400-g) cans tomato juice
1 pint (600 ml) chicken stock
a good pinch basil
2 to 3 tablespoons chopped chives
salt
freshly ground black pepper
½ level teaspoon caster sugar
a little Worcestershire sauce
cucumber slices
a little single cream

Put the tomato juice, stock and basil in a saucepan and bring to the boil.

Remove from the heat and add chives, seasoning and sugar to taste. Turn the soup into a bowl, leave to cool and then chill in the refrigerator. Before serving check seasoning and add a little Worcestershire sauce if needed.

When ready to serve, divide the soup between 6 individual serving bowls and float slices of cucumber on top, with a swirl of cream.

Serves 6

Chilled Avocado Soup

This makes 1 large avocado serve 4 people. Serve in small bowls with hot brown bread rolls.

Preparation time about 5 minutes
Chilling time about 1 hour

1 large avocado
15-oz (425-g) can consommé
5 tablespoons soured cream or single cream
salt and pepper
1 tablespoon lemon juice

Remove the stone from the avocado pear and scoop out the flesh. Place in a blender or processer with the can of consommé and reduce to a purée.

Turn into a bowl, add the cream, salt, pepper and lemon juice and then cover with cling film and chill in the refrigerator (the soup may discolour slightly).

Taste and check seasoning and then ladle into small soup bowls.

Serves 4

Gaspacho

You can use 1 lb (450 g) fresh tomatoes if they are cheap and plentiful, but skin them first.

Preparation time about 15 minutes
Chilling time about 1 hour

15½-oz (425-g) can peeled tomatoes
1 small onion, sliced
1 clove garlic, crushed
2 slices white bread, crusts removed
4 tablespoons wine vinegar
6 tablespoons corn or vegetable oil
½ pint (300 ml) chicken stock
¼ small green pepper, seeded and diced
1 to 2 tablespoons lemon juice
salt and pepper
¼ cucumber, diced
fried bread or croûtons (see page 187)

Put the tomatoes, onion, garlic, bread, vinegar, oil and stock in the blender or processor and purée for a few seconds.

Turn into a bowl, add the green pepper, lemon juice and seasoning and chill well.

Serve garnished with diced cucumber and croûtons.

Serves 4

MEAT STARTERS

With a good stock of packed sliced meats from the delicatessen in the fridge – ham, liver sausage, garlic sausage, salami – you need never be at a loss for a quick lunch or supper dish. It can be served with salad, or preceded by soup, depending on the meal that you are planning.

Pâtés and terrines are invaluable and your own home-made ones are best of all. A blender or processor makes preparation easy. Chicken livers and bacon trimmings are economical ingredients, and don't forget that seasoning is important. Keep some pâté ready in the freezer or fridge and all you have to do is thaw or bring to room temperature, cut in slices and serve with crisp French bread or hot buttered toast, and a green salad, perhaps.

Fast Brandied Pâté

A real cheat pâté, but very good.

Preparation time about 5 minutes
Setting time about 30 minutes

4 oz (100 g) liver sausage
3 oz (75 g) rich cream cheese
2 tablespoons brandy
good pinch garlic salt
freshly ground black pepper
1 oz (25 g) butter, melted

Put the liver sausage and cream cheese together in a bowl and beat with a wooden spoon until smooth and blended. This can also be done using an electric or hand whisk. Beat in the brandy, garlic salt and freshly ground black pepper.

Turn into a small dish and smooth the top, pour over the melted butter and leave in a cool place to set. Serve with hot toast and butter.

Serves 4

Brandied Chicken Pâté

A first-rate pâté which is lovely for a dinner party garnished with cucumber and radish slices. Make it in advance and keep it in the fridge for a week, or in the freezer for up to a month. *(Illustrated on the jacket.)*

Preparation time about 10 minutes
Cooking time about 1½ hours

    6 rashers streaky bacon, rind removed
    1 egg
    4 oz (100 g) white bread, crusts removed
    4 tablespoons brandy
    1 lb (450 g) chicken livers
    1 clove garlic, crushed
    salt and freshly ground black pepper
    scant level teaspoon nutmeg
    4 oz (100 g) bacon trimmings, cut in small pieces
    4 oz (100 g) lard, melted

Heat the oven to 325°F, 160°C, gas mark 3. Stretch the 6 rashers with the back of a knife on a board, then use them to line the base and the sides of a 2 pint (a good litre) loaf tin or deep pie dish.

Put the egg into the processor or blender with the bread broken into small pieces, brandy and half the chicken livers. Purée and turn into a bowl. Next put the garlic, remaining chicken livers, seasoning, nutmeg and bacon trimmings in the blender and purée. Add to the first batch of mixture. Stir in the melted lard, mix thoroughly and pour into the dish or tin.

Cover with foil and place the dish or tin in a meat tin containing an inch (2.5 cm) warm water. Bake in the oven for about 1½ hours. The pâté is cooked if the juices run clear when the centre is pricked with a skewer. Remove the pâté from the oven and leave to become quite cold before turning out onto a serving dish.

Serves 10

Potted Bacon

This is a good way to use up the last of a large bacon joint. Serve with hot toast and butter. It will keep for up to a week in the refrigerator. *(See picture facing page 64.)*

Preparation time about 10 minutes
Chilling time about 2 hours

12 oz (350 g) lean cooked bacon, minced
4 oz (100 g) butter, melted
4 tablespoons double cream
1 tablespoon fresh chopped parsley
1 teaspoon made mustard
2 tablespoons sherry
pinch ground nutmeg
freshly ground black pepper

Mix the bacon with half of the melted butter, then add the remaining ingredients and mix to a smooth paste. Press into 6 small soufflé dishes or ramekins.

Pour over the remaining melted butter to seal, then keep in the refrigerator until required.

Serves 6

Baked Ham Rolls

This recipe is very good served as a lunch or supper dish with slices of granary bread or bread rolls.

Preparation time about 10 minutes
Cooking time about 20 to 25 minutes

6 slices ham
10-oz (280-g) can green asparagus spears, drained

Cheese sauce
1 oz (25 g) butter
1 oz (25 g) flour
½ pint (300 ml) milk
2 oz (50 g) Cheddar cheese, grated
½ teaspoon made mustard
salt and pepper

Heat the oven to 400°F, 200°C, gas mark 6. Lightly butter a shallow ovenproof serving dish.

Lay the slices of ham flat and divide the asparagus evenly between the slices (about 4 spears to each slice of ham). Roll up and lay in a single layer in the dish.

To make the sauce, melt the butter in a saucepan, stir in the flour and cook for a minute. Blend in the milk and bring to the boil, stirring, until the sauce has thickened. Stir in most of the cheese, the mustard, salt and pepper to taste. When the cheese has melted, taste sauce to check seasoning, and then spoon over the ham. Sprinkle with the remaining cheese, put in the oven and cook for 20 to 25 minutes until the top is golden brown and bubbling.

Serves 6 as a first course and 3 as a lunch or supper dish

Ham Cornets

For this you need to have well shaped, thinly sliced ham. Serve with hot rolls.

Making time about 5 minutes

3 oz (75 g) white cabbage, finely shredded
1 stick celery, chopped
2 spring onions, thinly sliced
1 oz (25 g) sultanas
2 tablespoons corn oil
1 tablespoon vinegar
1 tablespoon mayonnaise (see page 178)
salt
freshly ground black pepper
4 slices ham

Blend together the cabbage, celery, onion, sultanas, oil, vinegar, mayonnaise and seasoning in a bowl, making sure that everything is well mixed.

Divide the mixture between the four ham slices and roll up to form a cornet shape. Place on a serving dish.

Serves 4 for a first course but would serve 2 for lunch or salad supper

Salami Jumble

This is a good first course to serve before a salad.

Making time about 10 minutes

6 oz (175 g) tagliatelle
2 oz (50 g) butter
4 oz (100 g) button mushrooms, sliced
4 oz (100 g) salami, cut in strips
4 oz (100 g) frozen peas, sweetcorn and peppers, cooked
salt
freshly ground black pepper

Cook the tagliatelle in plenty of fast boiling salted water until just soft as directed on the packet (about 5 minutes). Drain thoroughly, then rinse in warm water and drain again.

While the tagliatelle is cooking, melt the butter in a good sized saucepan, add the mushrooms and cook for 2 to 3 minutes, then stir in the salami and peas, corn and peppers. Heat through.

Add the tagliatelle and mix in well with a wooden fork. Add salt and plenty of freshly ground black pepper, and serve very hot.

Serves 4 to 6

Pasta alla Carbonara

Add the egg and cream mixture to the pasta just before serving, heat through and serve at once.

Making time about 20 minutes

   8 oz (225 g) bow-tie pasta
   3 oz (75 g) butter
   1 tablespoon corn or vegetable oil
   4 to 6 oz (100 to 175 g) back bacon, cut in strips
   1 onion, finely chopped
   3 egg yolks
   6 tablespoons single cream
   3 oz (75 g) Cheddar cheese, finely grated
   freshly ground black pepper
   salt

Cook the pasta as directed on the packet for about 11 minutes in fast boiling salted water or until tender. Rinse and drain thoroughly.

Meanwhile melt the butter in a large saucepan, add the oil and when hot, add the bacon and onion. Cook gently for about 10 minutes until the onion is soft but not brown. Blend the yolks with the cream and 2 oz (50 g) of the cheese.

Stir the pasta into the bacon and onion, pour in the cream mixture and toss very lightly with a fork to cook the mixture gently over a low heat. Do not over-cook the sauce or it will scramble.

Taste and check seasoning and add plenty of freshly ground black pepper and a little salt if necessary. Pile onto a serving dish and sprinkle with the remaining cheese.

Serves 4

Pasta and Chicken Scallops

These make a delicious first course, ideal to serve before a salad or light meal. *(See picture facing page 65.)*

Preparation time about 10 to 15 minutes
Cooking time about 5 minutes

6 oz (175 g) quick-cook shortcut macaroni
water
salt
3 tablespoons oil
1 large onion, chopped
4 rashers back bacon, chopped
6 oz (175 g) button mushrooms, sliced
about 7 fl oz (200 ml) double cream
6 oz (175 g) cooked chopped chicken
2 tablespoons chopped parsley
salt and pepper
4 tablespoons fresh white breadcrumbs
2 oz (50 g) Cheddar cheese, grated
4 small sprigs of parsley

Cook the macaroni in a large pan of boiling water with plenty of salt and a tablespoon of oil for about 8 minutes until just tender, or as directed on the packet. Drain well.

Meanwhile fry the onion in the remaining oil for 2 minutes. Add the bacon and mushrooms and cook for a further 3 to 4 minutes. Stir in the cream, chicken, parsley and macaroni and season well.

Spoon into 4 greased scallop shells or small individual ovenproof dishes. Sprinkle with breadcrumbs and grated cheese. Brown under a moderate grill for about 5 minutes.

Garnish each scallop with a sprig of parsley.

Serves 4

Rice Timbales

Serve a little extra French dressing and coarsely chopped parsley with the timbales. If you haven't dariole or castle tin moulds use small tea cups instead.

Making time about 20 minutes

6 oz (175 g) long-grain rice
6 oz (175 g) ham, cut in thin strips
7-oz (200-g) can sweetcorn, drained
4 oz (100 g) cooked peas
6 tablespoons French dressing (see page 179)
salt and pepper
chicory leaves to garnish

Cook the rice in plenty of boiling salted water until tender, about 12 minutes or as directed on the packet. Rinse well with warm water and drain very well.

When the rice is as dry as possible, place in a large bowl and stir in the ham, sweet corn, peas and dressing and mix very well. Add seasoning to taste. Brush 6 dariole moulds of ¼ pint (150 ml) capacity with oil and divide the mixture between them, pressing the rice in firmly.

Leave in a cool place until required and then turn out onto individual plates and garnish each with chicory leaves.

Serves 6

FISH STARTERS

Fish is a first course that most people enjoy and it is a boon to the cook. For one thing, cooking time is short. For another, you do not have to use expensive fish. Smoked salmon pieces or canned salmon make excellent mousses and creams, lemon sole is much cheaper than Dover sole and can take its place in most dishes. Canned crab and canned tuna fish from the store cupboard are good standbys. Smoked mackerel makes an excellent pâté and smoked haddock is the basis of a delicious mousse.

Most people immediately think of shellfish as prawns, crab or shrimps, but don't overlook cockles, mussels and scallops, which taste wonderful and are infinitely adaptable.

When you are using fresh fish, do make sure that it is really fresh. And remember that more expensive fish can be stretched with other ingredients – mushrooms, avocado, melon, cream, potato.

Tuna Pâté

Tuna is a very versatile fish and there is no need to have a blender or processor for this rough pâté.

Preparation time about 10 minutes
Chilling time about 1 hour

    1 oz (25 g) butter
    1 small onion, chopped
    2 × 7-oz (200-g) cans tuna fish, drained
    1 teaspoon anchovy essence
    2 teaspoons vinegar
    6 oz (175 g) soft butter
    salt and pepper

Melt the butter in a small saucepan, add the onion and cook gently for 5 minutes or until soft.

Mash the tuna fish in a bowl with a fork until smooth and then stir in the onion and all the other ingredients and mix very well. Taste and check seasoning.

Turn into a 1½ pint (900 ml) dish or terrine and chill before serving, with hot toast and butter.

Serves 6

Smoked Mackerel Pâté

This fish pâté can also be made using smoked trout, when it will have a milder flavour.

Preparation time about 10 minutes
Setting time about 30 minutes

   2 smoked mackerel
   10 oz (275 g) butter, melted and cooled
   4 oz (100 g) cream cheese
   juice of half a lemon
   salt and black pepper

Take the skin off the mackerel and remove any bones that may be present. Put the fillets with 8 oz (225 g) of the butter, the cream cheese and lemon juice in to the blender or processor in 2 batches and purée until smooth. Season with a little salt and pepper to taste.

Divide the pâté between 6 individual serving dishes and smooth the tops. Spoon a little of the remaining melted butter over the top of each dish and then leave until set. Serve with hot toast and butter.

Serves 6

Brandade of Kipper

To get a really smooth result you do really need a blender or processor. Keep in the refrigerator for 3 to 4 days.

Preparation time about 20 minutes
Chilling time about 1 hour

> 6-oz (175-g) packet frozen buttered kipper fillets
> 2 teaspoons lemon juice
> 5 tablespoons single cream
> 5 tablespoons double cream, whipped
> salt and pepper

Cook the kipper fillets in the bag according to the instructions on the packet. Then open the bag, pour off the juices and reserve, and take the skins from the kipper fillets.

Put the kippers in a blender or processor with the juices and purée until smooth. Turn into a bowl and when cold, stir in the lemon juice and single cream and mix until smooth. Fold in the double cream and taste and add seasoning.

Divide between 6 individual ramekins and chill for about an hour before serving. Serve with hot toast and butter.

Serves 6

Taramasalata

This smoked cod's roe pâté comes from Greece, and makes a good first course that is a little different.

Preparation time about 15 minutes
Chilling time about 1 hour

  8 oz (225 g) smoked cod's roe
  2 small slices white bread, crusts removed
  2 tablespoons milk
  1 clove garlic, crushed
  ¼ pint (150 ml), less 2 tablespoons, corn or vegetable oil
  2 tablespoons lemon juice
  salt and pepper

Remove the skin from the cod's roe, place in a processor or blender and purée until smooth.

Soak the bread in the milk, then squeeze out as much milk as is possible, and add bread to the blender with the garlic. Add the oil a teaspoonful at a time to the blender and purée until all has been absorbed, then blend in the lemon juice and seasoning to taste.

Turn into a small serving dish and chill well. Serve with hot buttered toast or with hot pitta bread, the traditional accompaniment.

Serves 4

Smoked Fish Pâté

Jars of taramasalata are sold in supermarkets and delicatessens. They should be kept in the fridge once you get home. If you have time, the same mixture is lovely thinned down to a piping consistency with more cream and piped on to fried bread croûtons and served with pre-dinner drinks. Alternatively, serve it as a quick savoury dip for biscuits and crudités. Brands of taramasalata do vary and you may find the recipe is improved by adding a little fresh lemon juice.

Making time about 5 minutes

6-oz (175-g) jar taramasalata (or see previous page)
4 oz (100 g) cream cheese
salt and pepper
4 tablespoons double cream

Put all the ingredients together in a bowl and mix thoroughly. Taste and check seasoning and then pile into a ½ pint (300 ml) dish.

Serve with hot toast and butter.

Serves 4

Smoked Haddock Mousse

This makes a delicious first course for 6 to 8 people, but would happily serve 4 for a lunch party.

Preparation time about 25 minutes
Setting time about 1 hour

1 lb (450 g) smoked haddock
½ pint (300 ml) milk
freshly ground black pepper
1 oz (25 g) butter
¾ oz (19 g) flour
½ oz (1 packet) powdered gelatine
2 tablespoons water
½ pint (300 ml) mayonnaise (see page 178)
juice of 1 lemon
¼ pint (150 ml) double cream, whipped
2 hard-boiled eggs, finely chopped
cucumber slices to garnish

Place the fish in a shallow pan, pour over the milk and season with black pepper. Poach gently for about 10 minutes or until the fish flakes easily. Drain the fish, reserving the milk, then flake the fish and remove all skin and bones.

Melt the butter in a saucepan, stir in the flour, cook for a minute, then add the flavoured milk and bring to the boil, stirring, until thickened. Place the gelatine in a small bowl with the water and leave to soak for a few minutes, then add to the hot sauce and stir until dissolved.

Put the white sauce and flaked fish in a blender or processor and purée until smooth. Turn into a large bowl and when cool, stir in the mayonnaise and lemon juice. Fold in the cream and chopped eggs.

Taste and check seasoning and turn into a 2 pint (1 litre) serving dish. Leave in a cool place to set, then decorate with slices of cucumber before serving.

Serves 6

Chilled Melon with Prawns

The great must of this recipe is to mix the prawns and melon with the cream at the very last moment otherwise you end up with a runny mess. As a variation add a little curry powder and a dash of mango chutney juice from the jar.

Making time about 10 minutes

1 ripe melon, well chilled
4 oz (100 g) shelled prawns
¼ pint (150 ml) soured cream
salt
freshly ground black pepper
small sprigs of mint

Cut the melon in half, then scoop out the flesh in balls using a small potato scoop. If you do not have a scoop, the flesh may be cut into ½ inch (1.25 cm) cubes.

Divide the melon balls between 4 individual serving dishes and sprinkle them with the prawns.

Season the soured cream with a little salt and plenty of freshly ground black pepper, and pour over the prawns and melon just before serving. Decorate each dish with mint sprigs.

Serves 4

Prawn Cocktail

This prawn cocktail is a little different, with added horseradish cream.

Making time about 10 minutes

6 oz (175 g) shelled prawns, plus 4 to 6 whole prawns to garnish
small lettuce, shredded

Sauce
¼ pint (150 ml) mayonnaise (see page 178)
2 tablespoons bottled horseradish cream
1 teaspoon tomato purée
a good pinch caster sugar
1 tablespoon lemon juice
2 tablespoons double cream
salt
freshly ground black pepper

Mix the prawns with the lettuce and divide between 4 or 6 individual glasses.

Mix all the sauce ingredients together, check seasoning, and spoon over the prawns and lettuce. Garnish each glass with a whole prawn.

Serves 4 to 6

Fish and Prawn Mayonnaise

This may be made a day ahead and kept in the refrigerator. Serve in individual glasses as you would a prawn cocktail.

Preparation time about 20 minutes
Chilling time about 1 hour

13-oz (375-g) packet frozen haddock fillets
¼ pint (150 ml) cider and water, mixed equally
juice of half a lemon
salt and pepper
1 tablespoon chopped mint
1 tablespoon chopped parsley
6 tablespoons thick mayonnaise (see page 178)
2 oz (50 g) peeled prawns
a little lettuce
paprika

Put the fish fillets into a shallow pan with the cider and water. Cover and simmer for about 10 minutes or until the fish is tender, will flake easily and is milky white in colour.

Lift fish out of the pan retaining the liquor, discard the skin and bones and flake the fish. Place in a bowl with the lemon juice and seasoning, and when cold add the herbs, mayonnaise and prawns with 2 tablespoons of the retained fish liquor. Mix very well. Cover with cling film and chill in the refrigerator.

Place a little shredded lettuce in the base of 4 individual glasses and spoon the fish mixture on top. Sprinkle with a little paprika.

Serves 4

Prawn Stroganoff

Serve this in vol-au-vent cases or with hot herb bread *(see page 183)*.

Preparation time about 15 minutes
Cooking time about 10 minutes

1½ oz (40 g) butter
1 large onion, finely chopped
4 oz (100 g) button mushrooms, sliced
8 oz (225 g) shelled prawns
5 oz (150 ml) carton soured cream
salt and pepper
4 large (about 3 inch or 7.5 cm) vol-au-vent cases, cooked

Heat the oven to 400°F, 200°C, gas mark 6.

Melt the butter in a saucepan, add the onion, and cook slowly for 5 minutes until the onion is soft but not brown. Add the mushrooms and prawns to the pan and simmer for 2 to 3 minutes. Stir in the soured cream, bring to the boil, and season to taste.

Divide between the vol-au-vent cases, place on an ovenproof serving dish, and heat through in the oven for 10 minutes.

Serves 4

Right: Potted Bacon (page 47).

Prawn Provençal

If using frozen prawns thaw slowly on kitchen paper in a cool place, which helps them keep their flavour.

Making time about 12 minutes

1 oz (25 g) butter
1 small onion, chopped
1 clove garlic, crushed
1 lb (450 g) tomatoes, skinned, quartered and pipped
1 teaspoon chopped parsley
1 teaspoon chopped chives
1 tablespoon dry sherry (optional)
8 oz (225 g) peeled prawns
salt
freshly ground black pepper

Melt the butter in a saucepan, add the onion, and cook gently until soft but not brown (about 5 minutes). Stir in the garlic and tomatoes with the herbs and sherry if used, and simmer for about 5 minutes so that the tomatoes are soft but still retain their shape.

Add the prawns and seasoning to taste, and reheat until boiling point.

Serve with plain boiled rice or thinly sliced brown bread and butter.

Serves 4 for a first course or could serve 2 for a lunch or supper dish

Left: Pasta and Chicken Scallops (page 52).

Creamed Salmon with Prawns

This dish makes a nice first course before a cold meal or it would serve 3 people for a supper or lunch dish, with perhaps a crisp green salad.

Making time about 15 minutes

6 oz (175 g) pasta shells
1½ oz (40 g) butter
1½ oz (40 g) flour
¾ pint (450 ml) milk
1 tablespoon tomato purée
salt
freshly ground black pepper
7½-oz (212-g) can red salmon
4 oz (100 g) cooked green peas
4 oz (100 g) peeled prawns

Cook the pasta as directed on the packet in fast boiling salted water for about 11 minutes or until tender. Rinse and drain very thoroughly, and keep warm.

Meanwhile make the sauce. Melt the butter in a small saucepan, stir in the flour and cook for a minute. Add the milk and cream, and bring to the boil, stirring, until the sauce has thickened. Add the tomato purée, salt and black pepper.

Drain the liquor from the salmon into the sauce, then remove the black skin and any bones from the fish. Flake and stir into the sauce, with the peas and prawns. Bring to the boil and taste and check seasoning.

Divide the pasta between 6 warm individual serving dishes and spoon the sauce on top. Serve at once.

Serves 6

Smoked Salmon Flan

If you are in a hurry and can buy a ready-made flan case and smoked salmon pieces from the delicatessen, this is well worth making.

Preparation time about 5 minutes
Cooking time about 35 minutes

> *an 8 inch (20 cm) flan case, baked*
> *6 wedges of lemon*

Filling
> *4 oz (100 g) smoked salmon pieces*
> *freshly ground black pepper*
> *2 eggs, beaten*
> *4 tablespoons milk*
> *1/4 pint (150 ml) single cream*
> *1 tablespoon chopped chives*

Heat the oven to 350°F, 180°C, gas mark 4. Place the flan case on an ovenproof serving dish.

Lay the pieces of salmon in the flan and season with pepper. Blend all the remaining ingredients together and pour into the flan case.

Bake in the oven for about 35 minutes or until set and a pale golden brown. Serve with wedges of lemon.

Serves 6

Salmon Cream

This may be made and served in individual dishes for a first course or put in a large dish and served with a salad for lunch.

Preparation time about 15 minutes
Setting time about 1 hour

½ oz (12½ g) butter
1 level tablespoon flour
¼ pint (150 ml) milk
8-oz (227-g) can red salmon
2 level teaspoons gelatine
1 tablespoon tomato ketchup
2 teaspoons lemon juice
salt and pepper
¼ pint (150 ml) mayonnaise (see page 178)
cucumber slices to garnish

Melt the butter in a small pan, stir in the flour and cook for a minute. Add the milk and bring to the boil, stirring, until the sauce thickens, then simmer for 2 minutes.

Drain the liquor from the can of salmon and place in a small bowl or cup with the gelatine and leave to soak for 3 minutes. Remove the white sauce from the heat and stir in the gelatine mixture until dissolved. Add the ketchup, lemon juice, salt and pepper and mix well.

Remove any bones and black skin from the salmon and place in a processor or blender with the sauce and mayonnaise. Purée until smooth.

Divide the mixture between 4 individual serving dishes, ramekins or glasses, or put in a 1 pint (600 ml) serving dish. Smooth the tops and leave to set, then garnish with thin slices of cucumber.

Serves 4

Surprisingly Good Salmon Mousse

Canned pink salmon is fine for this mousse, served in small ramekins decorated with a sprig of parsley.

Preparation time about 15 minutes
Setting time about 1 hour

½ oz, 12½ g (1 packet) powdered gelatine
3 tablespoons cold water
7½-oz (213-g) can pink salmon
1 tablespoon lemon juice
7-oz (200-g) jar mayonnaise
¼ pint (150 ml) double cream
salt
freshly ground black pepper
sprigs of parsley to garnish

Place the gelatine and water in a small bowl and leave for 3 minutes to form a 'sponge'. Stand in a pan of simmering water and stir until dissolved and the gelatine is clear. Leave to cool.

Drain the salmon, flake and remove any pieces of black skin and bone. Place in a bowl with the lemon juice and mayonnaise and mix thoroughly. Stir in the gelatine.

Whisk the cream until thick and just forms soft peaks, and then fold into the salmon mixture with seasoning to taste.

Divide the mixture between 5 to 6 small ramekin dishes, smooth the tops and leave in a cool place to set. Garnish each dish with a small sprig of parsley and serve with brown bread and butter.

Serves 5 to 6

Creamed Sole in Mushroom Sauce

Lemon sole is far cheaper than Dover sole and fine for this recipe.

Preparation time about 5 minutes
Cooking time about 25 minutes

   3 large lemon soles
   freshly ground black pepper
   knob of butter
   10½ oz (300 g) can condensed mushroom soup
   about 2 tablespoons sherry
   1 tablespoon chopped parsley
   a few bunches of white grapes to garnish

Heat the oven to 350°F, 180°C, gas mark 4. Butter a shallow 2 pint (a good litre) ovenproof dish.

Ask your fishmonger to fillet the soles for you, cutting each fish into 4 fillets. Sprinkle each fillet with freshly ground black pepper and roll up, skin side inside. Arrange the fillets standing upright in the dish.

Put the undiluted soup into a small bowl and blend in the sherry and parsley, then pour over the fish. Cover with a lid or piece of foil and bake the fish in the oven for 25 minutes or until the fillets look white and curd-like, and the flesh flakes easily.

Remove the lid and serve the dish garnished with small bunches of grapes.

Serves 6

Devilled Crab

Make in individual ramekin or gratin dishes. Serve very hot.

Preparation time about 20 minutes
Cooking time 10 minutes

> *2 oz (50 g) butter*
> *1 small onion, very finely chopped*
> *¹/₂ small green pepper, seeded and finely chopped*
> *2 oz (50 g) flour*
> *³/₄ pint (450 ml) milk*
> *2 level teaspoons French mustard*
> *¹/₂ level teaspoon mustard powder*
> *1 tablespoon Worcestershire sauce*
> *2 tablespoons chopped parsley*
> *salt and pepper*
> *a large pinch cayenne pepper*
> *4 hard-boiled eggs, chopped*
> *7-oz (198-g) can crab meat, drained*
> *4 level tablespoons grated Parmesan cheese*

Melt the butter in a saucepan, add the onion and green pepper and fry over a low heat for 5 minutes until soft. Blend in the flour and cook for a minute. Stir in the milk and bring to the boil, stirring continuously until thickened. Add the mustards, Worcestershire sauce, parsley, salt, peppers and egg, and mix well.

Flake the crab, remove any bones, and stir into the sauce.

Heat the grill to moderate. Divide the crab mixture between 4 individual heatproof dishes, sprinkle the tops with Parmesan cheese, and place under the grill until golden brown and bubbling.

Serves 4

Herrings with Spiced Cream and Cucumber

Use either canned or Matjes herring or jars of herring bought from the delicatessen counter.

Preparation time about 15 minutes

Cucumber salad
>   *3 tablespoons corn or vegetable oil*
>   *2 tablespoons water*
>   *2 tablespoons vinegar*
>   *2 level teaspoons caster sugar*
>   *½ teaspoon freshly chopped dill*
>   *a good pinch salt*
>   *½ cucumber, thinly sliced*

Spiced cream
>   *2 teaspoons lemon juice*
>   *1 level teaspoon dry mustard*
>   *2 level teaspoons caster sugar*
>   *½ small onion, finely chopped*
>   *a good pinch salt and pepper*
>   *¼ pint (150 ml) double cream, lightly whipped*
>
>   *6 oz (175 g) herring fillets, drained*
>   *1 tablespoon chopped parsley*

Blend all the salad ingredients together except for the cucumber. Place the cucumber in a dish and pour over the oil mixture and leave to stand for 15 minutes.

Meanwhile, mix together the lemon juice, mustard, sugar, onion and seasonings, and when smooth, fold in the cream.

Half an hour before serving, drain most of the liquor from the cucumber and arrange on a flat dish or, if liked, on individual serving dishes. Arrange the herring fillets on top of the cucumber, then spoon on the spiced cream and sprinkle with chopped parsley.

Serves 6

Scallops au Gratin

Scallops are best from October to April. If they are a bit expensive you could use just 1 scallop per person and add 4 oz (100 g) sliced button mushrooms, sautéed first in butter.

Preparation time about 25 minutes
Cooking time about 5 minutes

8 scallops
8 tablespoons white wine or dry cider
1 oz (25 g) butter
1 oz (25 g) flour
½ pint (300 ml) milk
2 to 3 oz (50 to 75 g) grated cheese
1 egg yolk
2 tablespoons cream or top of the milk

Remove the scallops from their shells, wash thoroughly and remove the beards and any black parts. Place them in a pan with the wine and simmer gently for 8 minutes.

Meanwhile make the sauce. Melt the butter in a saucepan, blend in the flour and cook for a minute without browning. Slowly stir in the milk and bring to the boil, stirring until thickened.

Remove the scallops from the pan with a slotted spoon and boil the wine rapidly until it has reduced to 1 tablespoon. Stir this into the sauce with three-quarters of the cheese and beat until smooth. Blend the egg yolk with the cream and add this to the sauce, then season to taste. Reheat but do not boil the sauce.

Place a little sauce into 4 scallop shells, then cut each scallop into pieces and lay in the shells. Spoon over the remaining sauce. Heat the grill to moderate. Sprinkle the remaining cheese on top of the sauce and place under the grill for about 5 minutes until the cheese has melted and is golden brown and bubbling. Serve at once.

Serves 4

Scallops en Brochette

This is a lovely first course to serve before a light main meal. Or you could double up and serve for lunch or supper. Allow 1 skewer for a first course and 2 skewers for a main meal. Serve with rice and tartare sauce (*see page 178*). (*Illustrated on the jacket.*)

Preparation time about 15 minutes
Cooking time about 8 to 10 minutes

4 scallops
1 small onion, chopped
about 5 tablespoons cider, or to cover
salt and freshly ground black pepper
about 4 oz (100 g) thin rashers streaky bacon
1 green pepper, seeded
about 8 mushrooms (small flats or buttons)
a little oil

Remove any black pieces from the scallops and wash them to remove any sand. Put in a saucepan with the onion, cider to just cover, salt and pepper, and place over a gentle heat. Cook carefully for about 8 minutes or until the scallops are tender. Lift out with a slotted spoon onto a plate, cut off the orange roes and then cut each scallop in half horizontally. Remove the rind from the bacon and then stretch flat with the back of a knife. Cut each rasher into 3 pieces and wrap a piece of bacon around each piece of scallop.

Cut the green pepper into 1 inch (1.25 cm) pieces and trim the stalks of the mushrooms flat with the cap.

Heat the grill to moderate. Lightly oil 4 skewers and thread the scallops, mushrooms and green pepper pieces onto each skewer equally. Brush the packed skewers with more oil and then place under the grill and cook for about 8 to 10 minutes, turning regularly so that the bacon is evenly crisp and brown. Brush with a little extra oil during cooking if necessary. Arrange the skewers on a bed of rice and serve at once.

Serves 4

Coquilles St Jacques

If liked these may be made in advance and then kept in the refrigerator until required and reheated in the oven for about 15 to 20 minutes at 400°F, 200°C, gas mark 6.

Preparation time about 20 minutes
Cooking time about 5 minutes

6 scallops
½ pint (300 ml) dry cider
1 oz (25 g) butter
1 oz (25 g) flour
Salt and black pepper
4.62-oz (131-g) packet instant mashed potato
a few browned breadcrumbs
6 small sprigs of parsley

Remove the scallops from their shells, wash thoroughly and remove the beards and place them in a saucepan with cider. Bring to the boil and simmer gently for 8 minutes. Lift out the scallops with a slotted spoon and reserve the cooking liquor for the sauce. Cut the scallops in slices.

To make the sauce, melt the butter in a small saucepan, add the flour and cook for a minute. Remove the pan from the heat and blend in the scallop cooking liquor. Return the pan to the heat and bring the sauce to the boil, stirring until thickened. Simmer for a minute then add the scallops and seasoning to taste.

Make up the potato as directed on the packet (adding a little butter and ground black pepper), and form a border around each of the scallop shells. Fill the centres with a spoonful of the sauce, dividing the mixture equally. Sprinkle over the breadcrumbs and put under the grill at a moderate heat for about 5 minutes until a pale golden brown. Garnish each shell with a small sprig of parsley, and serve at once.

Serves 6

Scallop Spaghetti

Use shortcut spaghetti, and serve the dish immediately it is cooked.

Making time about 15 minutes

4 scallops
about 1 level tablespoon flour
4 oz (100 g) shortcut spaghetti
1 oz (25 g) butter
4 oz (100 g) cooked ham, cubed
2 eggs, beaten
1 tablespoon chopped parsley
salt and pepper
1 oz (25 g) grated Parmesan cheese

Wash and dry the scallops, cut each into quarters, and then toss in the flour. Cook the spaghetti in boiling salted water for about 10 minutes until tender, or as directed on the packet. Drain well, rinse in warm water and then drain again and return to the saucepan.

While the spaghetti is cooking, melt the butter in another saucepan and fry the ham and scallops for 5 minutes over a medium heat. Stir into the cooked, drained spaghetti using a fork. When piping hot, stir in the eggs, parsley and seasoning, reduce the heat and cook gently until the eggs have scrambled. Taste and check seasoning, turn into a warm serving dish, sprinkle with the Parmesan cheese and serve at once.

Serves 4

Moules Marinière

Make sure that every mussel is tightly closed before they are cooked. This means that they are all alive and there are no bad ones. This dish could also be made with fresh cockles. The tightly closed shells should be left in a bucket of lightly salted water for an hour, then scrubbed before proceeding as in the recipe.

Making time about 30 minutes

4 pints (2.3 litres) fresh mussels
1 oz (25 g) butter
1 onion, finely chopped
4 stalks parsley
2 sprigs fresh thyme
1 bayleaf
freshly ground black pepper
½ pint (300 ml) dry cider
salt
1 oz (25 g) butter creamed with ½ oz (12½ g) flour
chopped parsley

Scrape and clean each mussel with a strong knife to remove all seaweed, mud and beard. Wash thoroughly in several changes of water, then drain.

Melt the butter in a large saucepan over a low heat, add the onion and fry until soft but not coloured. Add the herbs, pepper, cider, salt and mussels, cover the saucepan with a tightly fitting lid and cook quickly, shaking the pan constantly until the mussels open (about 5 to 6 minutes). Lift the mussels out, discard the empty half shell, and keep warm in a covered dish.

Remove the herbs from the cooking liquor. Drop the creamed butter and flour into the stock a teaspoonful at a time and whisk until the sauce has thickened. Taste and check seasoning, pour over the mussels and serve sprinkled with chopped parsley.

Serves 4

Whitebait

These are small fish that are caught off the east coast of England and are always eaten whole.

Preparation time about 10 minutes
Cooking time about 6 to 10 minutes

1½ lb (675 g) whitebait
3 oz (75 g) seasoned flour
oil for deep frying
lemon wedges
parsley

Pick over the whitebait carefully and remove any that are damaged and any pieces of sea weed. These fish bruise easily so be careful and do not handle too much.

Toss the whitebait gently in the seasoned flour – best done by putting the flour in a plastic bag, adding the fish and shaking gently.

Heat the oil to 375°F, 190°C in a large fish fryer. If you haven't a thermometer, the correct temperature is reached when a cube of day-old bread is golden brown in 1 minute. Place the whitebait in the basket a few at a time and deep fry each batch for about 2 minutes until crisp and cooked through. Lift out and drain on kitchen paper.

Pile onto a warm serving dish and garnish with lemon wedges and sprigs of parsley. The parsley can also be deep fat fried for just a few seconds, which gives it added taste and crispness. Serve with thinly sliced brown bread and butter.

Serves 4

Crispy Kebab Sticks

Take care when lifting the kebabs in and out of the hot fat; use either tongs or a spoon and fork. *(See picture facing page 96.)*

Preparation time about 10 minutes
Cooking time about 3 to 4 minutes

1 lb (450 g) cod or haddock fillets, skinned and cubed
4 oz (100 g) mushrooms, halved
seasoned flour

Batter
4 oz (125 g) plain flour
pinch salt
1 level teaspoon dry English mustard
1 egg, separated
¼ pint (150 ml) water

oil for deep frying
lemon and tomato wedges

Dust the fish and mushrooms with flour and then arrange on metal skewers with a halved mushroom at each end and the fish in the centre.

For the batter, put the flour, salt and mustard in a bowl. Blend the egg yolk with the water and beat into the flour until smooth. Whisk the egg white until stiff and then fold into the batter.

Heat the oil to 375°F, 190°C. Spoon the batter over the kebabs and deep fry for 3 to 4 minutes. Lift out and drain on kitchen paper.

Arrange the kebabs on a serving dish and garnish with lemon and tomato wedges. Serve with either tartare sauce *(see page 178)* or fresh tomato sauce.

Serves 4

Lobster Newburg

This is a good way of serving lobster hot and makes 1 lobster serve 4 for a first course.

Making time about 10 minutes

1½ to 1¾ lb (675 to 800 g) lobster
1½ oz (40 g) butter
6 tablespoons medium sherry
¼ pint (150 ml) double cream
2 egg yolks
salt
freshly ground black pepper
cayenne pepper
4 small sprigs of parsley

Ask your fishmonger to split the lobsters and crack the claws. Remove the meat from the claws with a sharp knife.

Melt the butter in a shallow pan and add all the lobster flesh cut in pieces and cook gently for 4 minutes, turning once. Stir in the sherry and let the mixture simmer until the sherry is reduced to 2 table-spoons. Stir in all but 2 tablespoons of the cream and heat through until the mixture is just below boiling point.

Blend the remaining cream with the egg yolks and add this to the lobster mixture. Reheat carefully to thicken the sauce slightly, but do not allow to boil, as it will curdle.

Taste and season with salt and pepper, then divide the lobster between 4 warm individual serving dishes. Sprinkle each with a little cayenne pepper and garnish with a sprig of parsley.

Serves 4

VEGETABLE STARTERS

For simple and inexpensive first courses serve fresh vegetables in season when they are at their best and cheapest and need little cooking and few additions. Broad or French beans straight from the garden cannot be beaten for flavour, and leeks are at their best when they are small and tender. Mushrooms in a French dressing, tomatoes sliced with onions, globe artichokes or asparagus in melted butter are all light and easy and a happy prelude to the main course that follows.

When you are serving a fairly light main course, start the meal with something more substantial, like stuffed and baked tomatoes or aubergines, or cauliflower au gratin.

It is worth cooking more vegetables than you need, then they can be used *au gratin* next day. Or make ratatouille and serve it hot or cold at dinner and use the rest later to accompany a meat dish.

Crudités

Crudités are pieces of raw vegetables that are served with a mayonnaise type sauce as a dip, either as a first course or with drinks. For a dinner party it is nice to make two or three dips and put them in the centre of the table with a selection of vegetables and let people help themselves.

Making time about 20 minutes

2 carrots, peeled
1 onion
½ cucumber
2 to 3 sticks celery
1 small cauliflower
1 red and 1 green pepper
1 bunch radishes

Cut the carrots into strips about 2 to 3 inches (5 to 7.5 cm) along and ¼ inch (6 mm) square. Cut the onion into thin rings. Leave the peel on the cucumber and cut into wedges. Cut the celery into sticks like the carrots. Break the cauliflower into tiny sprigs, leaving a small piece of stalk on each so that they are easy to pick up. Cut the peppers into strips, removing all white pith and seeds. Wash the radishes and cut off the roots, leaving on about ¼ inch (6 mm) of the green stalk. Make 4 slicing cuts down into the radish from the root end, and then leave in a bowl of iced water to open like a flower.

Take a large flat dish and place a bowl of curry dip in the centre and arrange the vegetables in neat piles around it.

Curry Dip

To ½ pint (300 ml) mayonnaise add ½ to 1 level teaspoon curry powder, ½ level teaspoon made French mustard, 1 tablespoon mango chutney juice and a teaspoon of lemon juice. Mix well.

Serves 4–6

Buttered Sweetcorn

Enjoy fresh in season from July to September but frozen sweetcorn is also very good.

Allow 1 corn cob per person and about 1 oz (25 g) butter

Remove the leaves and silky tassels from the cobs and put them in a single layer in a shallow pan holding just enough boiling water to cover them. Cook for 5 to 10 minutes adding salt half way through the cooking time. The corn will be milky white in colour and the kernels soft and tender.

Drain and serve the cobs at once with slices of butter on top. Insert cob holders or small skewers each end of the corn with which to hold it, and be sure to provide plenty of napkins and finger bowls or if in the kitchen lots of kitchen paper!

Globe Artichokes

The largest of these come from France, but clever gardeners *can* succeed in England – although *I* find I get one glorious one and the rest on the plant end up rather small!

Preparation time about 5 minutes
Cooking time about 30 to 40 minutes

> *6 globe artichokes*
> *salt*
> *water*

Wash the artichokes well in salted water, and break off the end of the long stalk on each.

Place the artichokes in a large pan of boiling salted water, boil for 1 minute, and then simmer until the leaves can be pulled out easily (about 30 to 40 minutes). Drain in a colander.

Globe artichokes may be eaten hot or cold and are served whole on individual plates. Each person pulls the leaves off his own artichoke and dips the tips of the leaves into the sauce.

Quick Lemon Sauce to Serve with Artichokes

Making time about 5 minutes

> *3 egg yolks*
> *2 teaspoons wine vinegar*
> *2 teaspoons lemon juice*
> *4 oz (100 g) unsalted butter*
> *1/4 teaspoon salt*
> *pinch white pepper*

Put the egg yolks in a blender with the vinegar and lemon juice and blend on maximum speed for a few seconds.

Just before serving bring the butter to boiling point in a pan, switch blender to maximum speed for a few seconds and then slowly pour on the boiling butter; blend until thick, and add seasoning. Pour into a warmed sauce boat and serve at once.

Serves 6

Artichoke Hearts in French Dressing

A good standby. It tastes best when you add lots of fresh parsley and chives.

Making time about 5 minutes

2 × 7-oz (200-g) cans artichoke hearts, drained
¼ pint (150 ml) French dressing (see page 179)
chopped parsley and chives

Divide the artichoke hearts between 4 individual serving dishes and coat them with French dressing. Sprinkle with chopped parsley and chives. Serve with thinly sliced brown bread and butter.

Serves 4

Tomatoes Lucinda

Extremely simple, and it's best to use large beefsteak tomatoes if you can get them.

Making time about 15 minutes

> *6 beefsteak or very large tomatoes*

Filling
> *6 oz (175 g) demi-sel cheese*
> *5 tablespoons single cream*
> *1 clove garlic, crushed*
> *salt and pepper*
> *1 tablespoon chopped chives*
> *4 tablespoons French dressing (see page 179)*

Put the tomatoes in a saucepan of boiling water for 10 seconds, then drain and remove the skins. Cut a slice from the stem end of the tomatoes and remove the seeds with a teaspoon, leaving the tomato shells in one piece.

Blend together all the filling ingredients except for a few chives and the French dressing. Add salt and pepper to taste. Spoon the cheese mixture into the tomatoes and place on a serving dish.

Just before serving blend the remaining chives with the French dressing and spoon over the tomatoes.

Serves 6 as a first course, or 3 as a salad

Swiss Stuffed Tomatoes

Use the large beefsteak tomatoes which are full of flavour and look spectacular. *(Illustrated on the jacket.)*

Making time about 10 to 15 minutes

4 large firm tomatoes
8 oz (225 g) cottage cheese
2 pickled cucumbers, chopped
2 tablespoons sweet chutney, chopped
salt
freshly ground black pepper
watercress

Skin the tomatoes by plunging them into boiling water for about 10 seconds and then into cold water. The skins will peel off easily.

Place a tomato, stalk side down, on a wooden board and with a sharp knife make cuts almost through to the base of the tomato to form six petals. Open out the petals gently to form a flower shape. Carefully remove the seeds from the centre of each tomato

Mix together the cottage cheese, cucumber, chutney and seasoning to taste. Pile this mixture into the tomatoes, arrange each tomato on an individual dish, and garnish with watercress.

Serves 4 as a first course or with a selection of cold meats as a main course, or serves 2 as a light lunch or supper dish, ideal for vegetarians

Baked Stuffed Tomatoes

Pick large tomatoes for this recipe, beefsteak if you can get them.

Preparation time about 10 minutes
Cooking time about 20 minutes

4 large tomatoes
3 rashers streaky bacon
1 tablespoon corn or vegetable oil
1 oz (25 g) butter
1 small onion, chopped
2 oz (50 g) mushrooms, chopped
1 oz (25 g) fresh breadcrumbs
salt
freshly ground black pepper

Heat the oven to 350°F, 180°C, gas mark 4. Lightly butter a shallow ovenproof serving dish.

Cut the tomatoes in half horizontally. Scoop out the core and seeds, and roughly chop them. Place the empty tomato cases in the buttered dish.

Remove the bacon rind, discard, and chop the bacon finely. Heat the oil and butter in a frying pan and fry the bacon and onion for 3 to 4 minutes, then stir in the mushrooms and cook for a further minute. Stir in the breadcrumbs and fry until crisp and have absorbed the butter and oil, then add the tomato pulp and mix well. Add salt and freshly ground black pepper to taste.

Divide the mixture between the tomato cases and then bake for 20 minutes. Serve at once.

Serves 4

French Dressed Mushrooms

A very quick first course. Choose small, firm, white button mushrooms of good quality, as they are to be served raw.

Preparation time about 10 minutes
Chilling time about 2 hours

8 oz (225 g) button mushrooms
¼ pint (150 ml) French dressing (see page 179)
a little chopped parsley

Wipe the mushrooms, trim the stalks level with the caps and slice very finely (keep the stalks to use in another recipe).

Put the mushrooms in a bowl, pour the dressing over and toss well. Cover and leave in a cool place for about 2 hours.

Turn into a serving dish and sprinkle with chopped parsley.

Serves 4

Mushrooms à la Grecque

Choose small white button mushrooms for this recipe, that is equally good served hot or cold. Keep the stalks and add to your next soup, casserole or risotto.

Making time about 15 minutes

> 1 lb (450 g) button mushrooms
> 4 tomatoes, skinned, seeded and chopped
> 4 tablespoons corn or vegetable oil
> ¼ pint (150 ml) white wine or cider
> 1 clove of garlic, crushed
> freshly ground black pepper
> salt

Trim the stalks of the mushrooms level with the caps. Place all the ingredients in a saucepan and bring to the boil. Cover the pan with a tight fitting lid, reduce the heat and cook gently for 5 minutes.

Lift out the mushrooms with a slotted spoon and place in a serving dish. Boil the wine or cider mixture rapidly for 2 to 3 minutes so that it reduces a little, and then taste and check seasoning and pour over the mushrooms.

Either eat at once or leave to become quite cold. Serve with chunks of French bread to soak up the juices.

Serves 4

Garlic Mushrooms with Cream

You need really small, fresh, white button mushrooms for this dish, otherwise the creamy sauce will be grey. Cook just before you serve – no problem as it takes just 10 minutes.

Making time about 12–15 minutes

  12 oz (350 g) small button mushrooms
  1½ oz (40 g) butter
  1 fat clove garlic, crushed
  salt
  freshly ground black pepper
  ¼ pint (150 ml) double cream

Wash the mushrooms and trim the ends off the stalks. Melt the butter in a large frying pan or saucepan and add the garlic and mushrooms and cook for 5 minutes.

Season well, stir in the cream and simmer gently for a further 5 minutes or until the mushrooms are tender. Divide between 4 ramekins or small dishes and serve hot with cheese bread rolls *(see page 181)*.

Serves 4

Stuffed Mushrooms

These make a simple light starter before a substantial main course.

Making time about 10 minutes

8 large flat mushrooms
2 oz (50 g) butter
2 rashers lean bacon, cut in strips
2 eggs
2 tablespoons milk
salt and pepper
4 slices buttered toast
4 sprigs parsley

Remove the stalks from the mushrooms and chop the stalks finely. Melt the butter in a frying pan and fry the whole mushrooms lightly on both sides. Lift out, draining off any butter, and keep warm. Add the mushroom stalks and bacon strips to the butter in the pan and fry for 3 to 4 minutes, stirring.

Beat the eggs, milk and seasoning together, pour into the pan with the bacon and stalks, and lightly scramble.

Place 2 mushrooms on each slice of buttered toast and divide the egg mixture between the mushrooms. Garnish with a sprig of parsley and serve at once on warm plates.

Serves 4

Mushrooms Stuffed with Cheshire Cheese

These could also be served as a savoury at the end of a dinner party or for a light lunch dish. *(See picture facing page 97.)*

Preparation time about 10 minutes
Cooking time about 20 minutes

 8 to 12 large flat mushrooms
 1 tablespoon melted butter
 salt and freshly ground black pepper
 1 oz (25 g) butter
 1 small onion, very finely chopped
 1 tablespoon flour
 ¼ pint (150 ml) single cream
 3 level tablespoons chopped parsley
 6 oz (175 g) Cheshire cheese
 small sprigs of parsley to garnish

Heat the oven to 375°F, 190°C, gas mark 5. Lightly butter an ovenproof dish. Remove the mushroom stalks and reserve. Brush the mushroom caps with melted butter and season well with salt and freshly ground black pepper. Lay in the base of the ovenproof dish.

Chop the mushroom stalks finely. Melt the 1 oz (25 g) butter in a frying pan and fry the mushroom stalks and onion gently for about 2 minutes. Stir in the flour and cook for a minute. Remove the pan from the heat and stir in the cream. Return to the heat and simmer until reduced and thickened. Season well and stir in the parsley. Divide the mixture between the mushroom caps and bake in the oven for 15 minutes. Heat the grill to moderate.

Remove from the oven and sprinkle with grated cheese. Place under the grill for about 3 to 5 minutes until the cheese has melted and is bubbling. Serve at once garnished with small sprigs of parsley.

Serves 4 to 6

Deborah's Mushrooms

These are very easy to prepare. I have filled them with a smooth liver pâté, but you could ring the changes by using a fish pâté or any smooth firm mixture.

Preparation time about 10 minutes
Cooking time about 4 minutes

about 3 oz (75 g) smooth liver pâté
8 oz (225 g) button mushrooms (probably about 32)
16 wooden cocktail sticks

Batter
2 oz (50 g) plain flour
a good pinch salt
about 4 tablespoons water
deep fat or oil for frying
tomato wedges and watercress to garnish

Put the pâté in a small bowl and beat with a wooden spoon until soft. Remove the stalks from the mushrooms (keep to use in a sauce or casserole), sandwich 2 mushrooms together with a small amount of pâté, and secure with a wooden cocktail stick. Repeat with the remaining mushrooms and pâté.

Put the flour for the batter in a bowl with the salt and beat in the water to make a thick coating batter. Heat the fat or oil until hot to 375°F, 190°C.

Dip each pair of mushrooms into the batter and then drop into the hot fat. Cook over a moderate heat until golden brown and crisp (about 4 minutes). Lift out and drain on crumpled kitchen paper, and remove the cocktail sticks.

Serve at once, allowing 4 stuffed mushrooms per person, and garnish with tomato wedges and a sprig of watercress.

Serves 4

Hot Asparagus

Simple and so delicious, the season for the English asparagus is May, June and July. Sprue asparagus (the thin spindly grade) is always cheaper than the best thicker stems, but tastes as good – you just have to eat more! Traditionally, asparagus is cooked in a deep, small-necked asparagus pan. Doing it this way uses a lot of water, but the heads cook at a slower rate than the stalks. I have found that my way of cooking asparagus, in a shallow pan or a frying pan with a tightly fitting lid, works very well. Alternatively, take a tip from a friend and use a coffee pot!

Preparation time about 5 minutes
Cooking time about 10 minutes

1 lb (450 g) asparagus
salt
4 oz (100 g) butter, melted

Cut off the woody ends of the asparagus, tie in three bundles and lay them in a shallow pan. Add about a teaspoon salt, cover with boiling water and then bring back to the boil and simmer for about 10 minutes or until tender.

Drain well, remove the string, place in a serving dish and serve at once with melted butter.

Serves 4

Broad Beans with Crispy Bacon

If fresh broad beans are unobtainable, use frozen, then this recipe can be prepared all the year round.

Preparation time about 15 minutes
Cooking time 5 minutes

1 lb (450 g) shelled broad beans
salt
4 to 8 rashers streaky bacon

Sauce
1 oz (25 g) butter
1 oz (25 g) flour
¾ pint (450 ml) milk
2 tablespoons chopped parsley
salt and pepper

Cook the beans in boiling salted water for about 6 minutes or until tender, drain well. Remove the rind from the bacon.

While the beans are cooking make the sauce. Melt the butter in a small saucepan and stir in the flour and cook for a minute. Add the milk and bring to the boil, stirring, until the sauce has thickened. Add the parsley, beans and seasoning to taste.

Heat the grill to moderate and grill the bacon rashers for about 5 minutes until crisp. Put the hot beans into a serving dish, sprinkle the crumbled bacon rashers on top, and serve with hot French bread.

Serves 4

Right: Crispy Kebab Sticks (page 79).

Ratatouille

This is a very versatile recipe to be served either hot or cold as a first course. It may also be served as a vegetable as an accompaniment to meat such as roast chicken or simple grills.

Making time about 35 minutes

4 tablespoons corn or vegetable oil
1 red pepper, seeded and cut into thick strips
1 green pepper, seeded and cut into thick strips
2 onions, sliced
2 courgettes, sliced
8 oz (225 g) tomatoes, skinned, quartered and seeded
salt and pepper

Heat the oil in a thick saucepan and add the peppers and onions. Fry for a minute, then cover, reduce the heat and cook gently for 20 minutes, stirring occasionally, until the onions are soft.

Add the courgettes and tomatoes with plenty of salt and pepper and cook without the lid for a further 10 to 15 minutes, until the courgettes are tender.

Taste and check seasoning and then serve either hot or cold with slices of French bread.

Serves 4

Left: Mushrooms Stuffed with Cheshire Cheese (page 93).

Aubergine Julius

Leave the skins on the aubergine as they become tender when cooked. To skin the tomatoes, drop into boiling water for a few seconds until the skin slips off easily when a small piece is touched with the point of a knife. Plunge at once into cold water, and remove the skins.

Preparation time about 35 minutes
Cooking time about 10 minutes

8 oz (225 g) aubergine
4 tablespoons corn or vegetable oil
1 large onion, sliced
3 tomatoes, skinned and sliced
salt and pepper
6 eggs
6 tablespoons single cream

Cut the aubergine into dice. Heat the oil in a saucepan, add the aubergine and onion, cover and cook gently for 20 minutes, then stir in the tomatoes and cook for a further 10 minutes.

Heat the oven to 350°F, 180°C, gas mark 4.

Remove the pan from the heat and season to taste. Divide the mixture between 6 individual ¼ pint (150 ml) ovenproof dishes and then break an egg into each dish. Spoon a tablespoon of cream over each egg, then place the dishes on a baking tray.

Cook in the oven for about 10 minutes or until the egg is set, with the white firm but the yolk still soft. Serve immediately with pieces of French bread.

Serves 6

Leeks au Gratin

Make this when the leeks are still small and tender, serving 1 per person.

Preparation time about 15 to 20 minutes
Cooking time about 5 minutes

4 leeks
salt
1 oz (25 g) butter
1 oz (25 g) flour
½ pint (300 ml) milk
3 oz (75 g) cheese, grated
freshly ground black pepper

Trim the roots and green parts from the leeks and wash very thoroughly. Cook in a pan of boiling salted water for 10 minutes or until the leeks are just tender. Drain very thoroughly, reserving 4 tablespoons cooking liquor, and then lay in a shallow 2 pint (a good litre) ovenproof dish and keep warm.

Melt the butter in a saucepan, stir in the flour and cook for a minute. Add the milk and bring to the boil, stirring, until the sauce has thickened. Blend in the leek cooking liquor and 2 oz (75 g) of the cheese, with plenty of freshly ground black pepper and extra salt if necessary.

Pour the sauce over the leeks, sprinkle with the remaining cheese and then place under medium grill for about 5 minutes until the cheese has melted and is golden brown.

Serves 4

Cauliflower au Gratin

I find this a popular first course when the main course is light. I keep breadcrumbs in the freezer so I just take out a couple of tablespoons for this dish. The rest I use for stuffings, charlottes, bread sauce etc.

Preparation time about 12 minutes
Cooking time about 5 minutes

> *1 cauliflower*
> *1 oz (25 g) butter*
> *1 oz (25 g) flour*
> *½ pint (300 ml) milk*
> *salt*
> *freshly ground black pepper*
> *a little made mustard*
> *2 oz (50 g) Cheddar cheese, grated*
> *1 level tablespoon Parmesan cheese, grated*
> *2 level tablespoons breadcrumbs*

Break the cauliflower into florets and cook in boiling salted water until barely tender (about 5 to 8 minutes). Drain well, reserving 4 tablespoons of the cooking liquor.

Melt the butter in a saucepan, stir in the flour and cook for a minute. Blend in the milk, reserved cooking liquor and seasonings, and bring to the boil, stirring, until the sauce has thickened. Simmer gently for 2 minutes, then add the Cheddar cheese. Stir until melted, then carefully stir in the cauliflower.

Divide between 4 individual serving dishes. Mix the Parmesan cheese with the breadcrumbs and scatter over the top. Put under a medium grill for about 5 minutes until crisp and brown.

Serves 4

Broccoli with Soured Cream Sauce

Take care not to boil the sauce – just heat until the yolks have thickened the cream.

Making time about 12 to 15 minutes

2 × 9-oz (250-g) packets frozen broccoli
¼ pint (150 ml) soured cream
2 egg yolks
½ level teaspoon made mustard
salt and pepper

Cook the broccoli according to the directions on the packet, drain, and arrange on 6 hot individual plates and keep warm.

Put the soured cream in a small pan and heat slowly to simmering point. Remove from the heat and pour onto the egg yolks and mix well. Add the remaining ingredients, then return the sauce to the pan and cook over a low heat for 2 minutes, stirring constantly until thickened. Pour over the broccoli just before serving.

Serves 6

Stuffed Courgettes

This makes a good hot first course in the summer. Courgettes and tomatoes are in season together and are always plentiful. Use the discarded flesh of the courgettes in a ratatouille or vegetable soup.

Preparation time about 15 minutes
Cooking time about 25 minutes

4 large courgettes
1 tablespoon oil
1 onion, finely chopped
2 oz (50 g) mushrooms, finely chopped
1 oz (25 g) fresh white breadcrumbs
4 tomatoes, peeled and finely chopped
salt
freshly ground black pepper

Heat the oven to 350°F, 180°C, gas mark 4. Lightly butter a shallow ovenproof dish.

Trim the ends from the courgettes and cut each in half lengthways. With a pointed spoon scoop out the centre to make a hollow for the filling. Put courgettes in a saucepan of boiling water and cook for 1 minute, then drain and lay in a single layer in the dish.

Heat the oil in a saucepan and fry the onion and mushrooms for 5 minutes, then stir in the breadcrumbs and tomatoes and cook for 2 to 3 minutes, mixing very well. Season and then divide the mixture between the courgettes. Cover the dish lightly with a piece of foil and bake in the oven for 25 minutes until courgettes are tender. Serve with French bread.

Serves 4

FRUIT STARTERS

A first course to be followed by a substantial main dish needs to be very light and appetising. Fresh fruit is ideal. It is quick and easy to prepare, refreshing to eat. A fruit starter may be hot (baked grapefruit for example) or very cold (grapefruit water ice), it may be a mixture of fruits, or it may be served with a special dressing.

Avocados make very quick first courses, served in a variety of different ways. For a quick store cupboard recipe, fill canned white peaches with pencil-thin strips of ham and celeriac mixed with mayonnaise. Pears, melons, apples and fresh peaches all make excellent starters.

Use fresh fruit in season when you can and make sure it is of the best quality.

Melon and Ginger Cocktail

This makes an attractive first course. If you like, you can dip the rims of the glasses in egg white and then into granulated sugar to give a frosted rim to the glasses. *(Illustrated on the jacket.)*

Preparation time about 10 minutes
Chilling time about 20 minutes

> *1 large honeydew melon*
> *4 oz (100 g) stem ginger, cut in small dice*
> *about 4 tablespoons ginger syrup*
> *caster sugar*
> *about 8 small sprigs of fresh mint*

Cut the melon in half and scoop out all the seeds. Cut the skin from the melon and then cut the flesh into neat ½ inch (1.25 cm) cubes. Put in a bowl with the stem ginger, ginger syrup and sugar, cover, and leave in a cool place for about 20 minutes for the flavours to blend.

Stir thoroughly, then divide between 8 glasses and decorate each glass with a small sprig of fresh mint.

Serves 8

Baked Grapefruit

There are many variations for baked grapefruit – try topping with mint jelly before grilling or bake in the oven with runny honey and nuts. This recipe combines grapefruit with ginger.

Preparation time about 5 minutes
Cooking time about 10 to 15 minutes

2 grapefruit
a small jar preserved ginger in syrup
4 teaspoons soft brown sugar

Heat the oven to 325°F, 160°C, gas mark 3.

Cut the grapefruit in half and cut around each half to loosen the flesh. Cut between the segments and remove any pith and white skin. Pour a tablespoon of the ginger syrup over each grapefruit half and sprinkle them with the sugar.

Cut the pieces of preserved ginger in thin slices and arrange around the edge of the grapefruit, and fill the centre cavity with small pieces of ginger. Place the grapefruit on an ovenproof dish and bake in the oven for 10 to 15 minutes until the sugar has dissolved and the grapefruit is hot through.

Serves 4

Grapefruit Water Ice

A refreshing sharp first course before a very substantial main course. It is quite quick to make, but is best prepared the day before it is needed.

Preparation time about 45 minutes
Freezing time about 1 hour
Thawing time 30 minutes

> *4 oz (100 g) caster sugar*
> *½ pint (300 ml) water*
> *6-oz (175-g) can frozen concentrated grapefruit juice*
> *3 egg whites*
> *a few mint sprigs*

Dissolve the sugar with the water in a pan over a low heat, then cool. Blend the thawed, undiluted grapefruit juice with the sugar syrup and pour into a shallow plastic container. Freeze for 30 minutes or until starting to set.

Turn into a bowl and mash until smooth, then fold in the stiffly whisked egg whites. Return to the container, cover and freeze until required.

Thaw in the refrigerator for about 30 minutes before serving. Serve in scoopfuls in glass dishes decorated with sprigs of fresh mint.

Serves 6

Florida Cocktail

Particularly suitable for those keeping an eye on their weight. For a change use some of the more unusual varieties of mini oranges, such as satsumas, clementines, wilkins or minolas.

Preparation time about 5 minutes
Chilling time about 1 hour

  2 grapefruit
  2 oranges

Cut the grapefruit in half and cut around each to loosen the flesh. Cut between the segments and remove any white skin and pith. Remove the flesh and put in a bowl, retaining the skins.

Peel the oranges with a serrated knife so that all the pith is removed, then divide the oranges into segments, removing the membrane between each segment.

Mix the fruit segments together and then pile back into the grapefruit halves. Chill well before serving.

Serves 4

Chilled Melon and Lime

Very refreshing and must be served very cold. Remember to allow an overnight 'maceration' in the refrigerator.

Preparation time about 10 minutes
Chilling time overnight

> *1 small ripe melon*
> *juice of 1 lime*
> *¼ pint (150 ml) sweet white wine*
> *4 sprigs of mint*

Halve the melon, remove and discard the seeds, and then remove the skin. Cut the flesh into neat ½ inch (1.25 cm) cubes. Put the cubes in a bowl with the lime juice and white wine, cover and leave overnight in the refrigerator.

Next day, stir well and then divide between 4 individual glasses and serve with a sprig of mint on each.

Serves 4

Melon and Tomato in Mint Dressing

A lovely fresh first course.

Preparation time about 15 minutes
Chilling time about 2 hours

1 honeydew or Galia melon
12 oz (350 g) firm tomatoes
1 cucumber
2 teaspoons mint jelly
1 tablespoon caster sugar
2 tablespoons wine vinegar
salt
freshly ground black pepper
6 tablespoons corn or vegetable oil
6 small sprigs of fresh mint

Cut the melon in half and remove the seeds. Either scoop the melon flesh out using a melon baller or peel, cut in wedges, and then cut the flesh into cubes.

Skin and quarter the tomatoes and remove the seeds (if the tomatoes are large cut each quarter in half). Peel the cucumber and cut into neat dice. Put cucumber, melon and tomatoes in a large bowl, and mix well together.

Melt the mint jelly in a saucepan with the sugar and vinegar, then remove from the heat and cool. Add seasoning and oil, mix, and pour over the fruits and toss well. Chill in a cool place, taste and check seasoning and then serve in glasses, garnished with a sprig of fresh mint.

Serves 6

Melon and Ham Gondolas

Sweet melon goes well with raw smoked Italian ham such as Parma, Serano or Prosciutto or a Westphalian ham from Germany. Slices can now be bought in vacuum packs from delicatessen counters of the best supermarkets. Choose the best buy in melons for the time of year.

Making time about 15 minutes

1 small chilled melon
6 thin slices smoked raw ham
juice of half a lemon
freshly ground black pepper
6 lemon wedges to garnish

Cut the melon into 6 wedges lengthwise and scoop out the seeds from each slice and cut off the skin.

Lay a melon wedge on each slice of ham and roll the ham around. Place on a serving dish and squeeze over the lemon juice. Season with black pepper, and garnish with lemon wedges.

Serves 6

Stuffed Pears Danish Style

Serve very cold. If you know that you are going to make these, cook extra bacon until crisp at breakfast time and use for the topping.

Making time about 15 minutes

3 fresh pears
juice of half a lemon
about 3 oz (75 g) Danish blue cheese
3 oz (75 g) rich cream cheese
crumbled crispy bacon
6 lettuce leaves

Peel the pears, cut in half lengthwise and scoop out the core with a teaspoon. Brush the pears with the lemon juice to prevent discoloration.

Crumble the Danish blue cheese. Place the cream cheese in a small bowl and cream until soft and then stir in the Danish blue, until well blended.

Divide this mixture equally between the pear halves. Place a leaf of lettuce on 6 individual serving dishes and put a pear half in the centre. Sprinkle over the crispy bacon and serve at once.

Serves 6

Fresh Fruit with Yogurt Dressing

Yogurt dressing goes well with salads too, as it is lighter and contains fewer calories. Do not mix the dressing with the fruit until the last moment because the juice of the fruit will make the sauce too runny.

Making time about 2 to 3 minutes

¹/₄ pint (150 ml) plain yogurt
3 to 4 tablespoons mayonnaise (see page 178)
selection of prepared mixed fruits

Place the yogurt in a bowl and stir in the mayonnaise until blended and smooth. Taste and add a little seasoning if you like, but this is not usually necessary.

Turn into a small dish and serve as a first course with a selection of prepared mixed fresh fruits, such as halved pipped grapes, sliced eating apples, cubed melon and pear.

Avocado with Caviar

Use either the red or black lumpfish roe – the poor man's caviar – or, if you are doing this for a larger number, put a small mound of red and black side by side for decoration.

Making time about 10 minutes

3 ripe avocados
juice of half a lemon
4 oz (100 g) cream cheese
2 to 4 tablespoons mayonnaise (see page 178)
salt and pepper
3 lettuce leaves, shredded
1½ oz (40 g) jar lumpfish roe

Peel the skins from the avocados. Cut in half and discard the stones, and then brush all over with lemon juice.

Mash the cream cheese in a bowl with a fork and then beat in the mayonnaise to make a smooth light consistency. Season and add any remaining lemon juice, and then pile into the hole in the avocado halves.

Divide the lettuce between 6 individual serving dishes and place an avocado half on each plate. Top each avocado with a little roe spooned in lines across the top.

Serves 6

Avocado Marie-Claire

This also makes an excellent salad, when you should slice the skinned avocado before mixing with the tomatoes. It goes well with cold rare roast beef.

Preparation time about 12 to 15 minutes
Chilling time about 30 minutes

2 firm tomatoes
2 tablespoons bottled mint jelly
5 tablespoons French dressing (see page 179)
1 spring onion, finely chopped
2 ripe but firm avocado pears
salt
freshly ground black pepper
4 sprigs fresh mint

Remove the tomato skins by dropping the tomatoes in boiling water for about 10 seconds. When the skin starts to loosen, plunge at once into cold water. Slip off the skins, halve the tomatoes, and remove all the pips and membrane (use for soups and sauces). Cut the tomato flesh into fine strips, and place in a small bowl.

Melt the mint jelly in a small saucepan over a low heat, then remove and add the French dressing and spring onion. Pour the mint dressing over the tomatoes, cover and chill until ready to serve.

When required for serving, cut the avocados in half and remove the stones. Taste the tomato mixture and if necessary add seasoning, then spoon into the avocado halves and decorate each with a sprig of mint.

Serves 4

Avocado and Citrus Salad

Make just before serving, otherwise assemble in a basin, toss in dressing and cover with cling film, then spoon out into dishes.

Making time about 15 minutes

2 grapefruit
2 thin skinned oranges
1 avocado pear
a little French dressing (see page 179)

Cut the grapefruit and oranges in half and cut around each to loosen the flesh. Cut between the segments and remove any white skin and pith. Peel the avocado pear, cut in half and remove the stone, and then cut the flesh into thin slices.

Put the grapefruit, orange and avocado into a bowl and add just enough French dressing to mix lightly. Divide between 6 glasses and serve at once with hot brown rolls.

Serves 6

Avocado Dip

A dip makes an interesting first course when there are just 4 people around a small table and everyone can easily stretch to the centre bowl. Serve with crudités of raw vegetables (*see page 82*).

Making time about 10 minutes

2 ripe avocado pears
5 tablespoons double cream
2 oz (50 g) cream cheese
½ level teaspoon dry mustard
2 level teaspoons caster sugar
2 tablespoons lemon juice
salt
freshly ground black pepper
green colouring (optional)
small sprig of watercress

Cut the avocadoes in half, and remove the stones. Scoop out the flesh, put in a bowl, and mash with a fork until smooth.

Blend together the cream and cream cheese and then stir into the avocado purée until well mixed. Season with the mustard, sugar, lemon juice and plenty of salt and pepper. Add a few drops of green colouring if required. Pile the mixture into a small serving dish and garnish with the sprig of watercress.

Serve with celery and cucumber sticks, cauliflower florets and carrot sticks, which are dipped into the avocado dip.

Serves 4

Avocado Creams

Make at least 6 hours in advance in order to let the ramekins set.

Preparation time about 10 minutes and 5 minutes
Cooling time about 1 hour

2 avocado pears
10½-oz (298-g) can condensed consommé
juice of half a lemon, or more to taste
salt and pepper
4 oz (100 g) streaky bacon

Peel the avocado pears, cut in half, remove the stones and put the flesh in a blender or processor. Purée with the consommé to a smooth consistency. Add lemon juice and seasoning to taste. Divide the mixture evenly between 6 ramekin dishes and leave in a cool place to set.

Remove the bacon rind, discard, and fry the bacon without any extra fat until crisp and golden brown on both sides. Lift out and leave to drain on a piece of kitchen paper. When cold snip with a pair of kitchen scissors into small pieces. Scatter over the avocado creams before serving with herb bread or toast.

Serves 6

Avocado and Prawn Creams

This recipe is ideal for a special dinner party. If the ingredients are all prepared and ready it can be made very quickly, just before serving.

Making time about 5 minutes

3 avocado pears
juice of 1 small lemon
¼ pint (150 ml) soured cream
about 3 tablespoons mayonnaise (see page 178)
a little salt
a good pinch cayenne pepper
4 oz (100 g) peeled prawns
6 whole prawns to garnish

Cut the avocado pears in half and remove the stones. Scoop out the flesh carefully (so as not to damage the skins), and put in a blender or processor with the lemon juice, soured cream, mayonnaise, salt and cayenne pepper. Purée until smooth, turn into a bowl, stir in the peeled prawns and taste and check seasoning.

Pile the mixture into the avocado skins and garnish each with a whole prawn in its shell. Serve with thinly sliced brown bread and butter.

Serves 6

BREAD, EGG AND CHEESE STARTERS

A substantial sandwich can be a lunch time or an evening snack; it goes well with home-made soup and somehow it is particularly good eaten in the open air. To taste good it must look good. Scandinavian open sandwiches are colourful, exciting to look at and nourishing as well. Use rye, granary or French bread, and butter it well. Then let yourself go and see what decorative and appetising results you can produce with tomato, cheese, pickles, prawns, anchovies, lettuce, eggs – whatever you have to hand.

Eggs and cheese are invaluable to the quick cook. They can be dressed up in innumerable ways and they combine with all manner of other ingredients as fast starters. Keep a good supply of both in store.

Open Sandwiches

An open sandwich goes well before a home-made soup on a cold day or vice versa. The best bread is the one that the Danes use – a firm rye bread which comes in packets already sliced – but otherwise choose a firm textured wholewheat or granary bread. The Danes are the experts on open sandwiches, but the Dutch also have a good one – called *Uitsmijter* – which you can get in restaurants all over the country at lunchtime.

Each sandwich will take about 5 minutes to prepare

Smoked Salmon and Egg *(Illustrated on the jacket.)*

For each sandwich you will need

> *knob of butter*
> *1 egg*
> *1 tablespoon milk*
> *salt and pepper*
> *2 teaspoons cream (optional)*
> *2 slices smoked salmon*
> *1 slice bread, thickly buttered*
> *chopped fresh dill (use parsley if unavailable)*

Melt a knob of butter in a saucepan. Beat the egg with the milk and seasoning, add to the pan and cook over a moderate heat, stirring until scrambled. Remove from the heat, stir in the cream and leave to cool.

Meanwhile lay a slice of smoked salmon on top of the bread, then spoon the scrambled egg on top. Roll up the remaining slice of smoked salmon and place on the eggs. Sprinkle with dill.

Vet's Midnight Snack *(See picture facing page 128.)*

For each sandwich you will need

1 slice liver pâté
½ slice rye bread, thickly buttered
2 slices salt beef or ham
2 onion rings
sprig of parsley

Arrange the liver pâté on the bread, roll up the beef or ham and put on top of the pâté. Place the onion rings on top and garnish with parsley.

Black and Blue *(See picture facing page 128.)*

For each sandwich you will need

1 crisp lettuce leaf
½ slice rye bread, thickly buttered
2 to 3 slices Danish blue cheese
3 halves of black grapes

Press the lettuce leaf on to the buttered bread. Arrange the cheese slices overlapping on top and decorate with grapes.

Crisp Bacon and Egg *(See picture facing page 128.)*

For each sandwich you will need

2 rashers streaky bacon
1 hard-boiled egg, sliced
½ slice rye bread, thickly buttered
1 slice tomato
watercress

Remove the rind from the rashers and fry bacon gently until crisp. Drain on kitchen paper. Arrange the egg in 2 rows on the bread so that it is completely covered, and lay the bacon on top. Cut the tomato slice through to the centre and form it into a twist. Place on top of the bacon, and decorate with watercress.

Pâté and Bacon Smörrebröd

For each sandwich you will need

1 rasher streaky bacon
1 slice rye bread, buttered
¾ oz (19 g) smooth liver pâté
half baby pickled dill cucumber, sliced

Remove rind and bone from the bacon and stretch rasher with the back of a knife. Cut in half and fry in a frying pan without any extra fat until crisp. Lift out with a slotted spoon and drain on kitchen paper.

Cut slice of bread in half and spread with pâté. Top with a slice of bacon and a couple of slices of dill cucumber. Serve on individual plates allowing 2 pieces per person.

Dutch Open Sandwich

For each sandwich you will need

1 slice bread, buttered
1 slice cooked ham
1 egg
1 tomato, sliced
a lettuce leaf

Place the bread on a plate, cover with a lettuce leaf and lay the ham on top. Fry the egg in a little butter and when cooked, lift out and place on top of the ham. Decorate with slices of tomato and serve at once with gherkins or pickle.

Leek and Cheese Quiches

These make a different starter and are ideal to hand around with drinks.

Preparation time about 20 minutes
Cooking time about 25 to 30 minutes

Pastry
8 oz (225 g) plain flour
½ level teaspoon salt
2 oz (50 g) butter
2 oz (50 g) lard
about 8 teaspoons cold water

Filling
1 oz (25 g) butter
1 medium leek, finely sliced
2 oz (50 g) Cheddar cheese, finely grated
1 egg, beaten
5 to 6 tablespoons single cream
salt and freshly ground black pepper

Heat the oven to 375°F, 190°C, gas mark 5.

Put the flour and salt into a bowl and rub in the butter and lard cut in small pieces. Add the cold water and mix to a firm dough. Roll out the pastry and cut into about 24 circles with a 3 inch (7.5 cm) cutter. Line small bun or tart tins, prick well, and bake blind for about 10 minutes.

Meanwhile, melt the butter in a small saucepan, add the leek and cook gently for 5 minutes until soft. Divide between the pastry cases with the cheese. Blend the egg with the cream and seasoning and pour into the pastry cases.

Return to the oven, reduce the heat to 350°F, 180°C, gas mark 4 and cook for 15 to 20 minutes until the filling is set and a pale golden brown. Serve either warm or cold.

Makes about 24 baby quiches

Quick Pizzas

Serve before or after a good soup on a Sunday night.

Preparation time about 5 minutes
Cooking time about 2 to 3 minutes

Salami and Mushroom Pizza

butter
4 oz (100 g) mushrooms, sliced
2 muffins
4 slices salami or liver sausage
4 pieces Emmenthal cheese

Melt a knob of the butter in a small saucepan, add the mushrooms and cook for 2 to 3 minutes. Heat the grill to moderate.

Split the muffins and toast on the cut side until golden brown, spread with butter and lay a slice of salami on each muffin. Top with the cooked mushroom mixture. Cover each with a slice of Emmenthal cheese and return to the grill for 2 to 3 minutes or until the cheese has melted and is golden brown and bubbling.

Serves 4

Tomato and Bacon Pizza

2 muffins, split
butter
3 tomatoes
freshly ground black pepper
4 green stuffed olives, sliced
4 rashers streaky bacon

Heat the grill to moderate and toast the muffins on the cut side until golden brown, spread with butter and increase the grill to hot.

Slice the tomatoes and divide between the muffins, season with freshly ground black pepper and cover with sliced olives. Remove the rind from the bacon, cut each rasher in half and place 2 pices of bacon on each muffin.

Return to the grill, cook for about 5 minutes, turning the bacon once so that it is cooked on both sides and the fat runs through to cook the tomatoes. Serve immediately.

Serves 4

Tomato and Cheese Pizza

1 onion, chopped
8-oz (227-g) can peeled tomatoes
good pinch mixed dried herbs
salt
freshly ground black pepper
4 muffins, split
about 2 oz (50 g) Cheddar cheese, grated

Put the onion, tomatoes, herbs and seasoning in a small saucepan and bring to the boil. Simmer gently for 5 minutes until the sauce has reduced and is thick. Meanwhile heat the grill to moderate and toast the muffins until golden brown.

Pile the tomato mixture onto the muffins – it is not necessary to butter them. Sprinkle with the Cheddar cheese and return to the grill and cook until the cheese has melted and is golden brown and bubbling. Serve at once.

Serves 4

Anchovy and Cheese Aigrettes

Only quick and easy if you have a deep fat pan on the go! Delicious served hot dusted with Parmesan cheese.

Preparation time about 15 minutes
Cooking time about 4 to 5 minutes

1 oz (25 g) butter
¼ pint (150 ml) water
2 oz (50 g) self-raising flour
1 egg yolk
1 egg
2 oz (50 g) mature Cheddar cheese, grated
2-oz (50-g) can anchovies, drained and finely chopped
pinch of cayenne pepper

Put the butter and water in a small saucepan and bring to the boil. Remove the pan from the heat and add flour. Beat well until the mixture is glossy and leaves the sides of the pan clean. Cool slightly.

Lightly mix the yolk and the egg together and beat into the mixture a little at a time. Stir in the cheese and the anchovies with a pinch of cayenne.

When required, drop the mixture in heated teaspoonfuls into hot deep fat (375°F, 190°C), and fry gently until golden brown, turning once.

Lift out with a slotted spoon and drain on kitchen paper. Pile into a warm serving dish and if liked dust with a little extra Parmesan cheese. Serve at once.

Makes 16 aigrettes

Individual Hot Cheese Soufflés

You can prepare these in advance and freeze covered with cling film, then almost thaw, and cook a little longer than the recipe.

Preparation time about 15 to 20 minutes
Cooking time about 20 minutes

1½ oz (40 g) butter
1½ oz (40 g) flour
½ pint (300 ml) milk
½ teaspoon made mustard
a large pinch nutmeg
2 oz (50 g) Cheddar cheese, grated
2 oz (50 g) Parmesan cheese, grated
3 large eggs, separated
salt and pepper

Heat the oven to 350°F, 180°C, gas mark 4. Use extra butter to grease 6 to 8 ramekins, depending on the size, and dust with extra Parmesan cheese, if you like.

Melt the 1½ oz (40 g) butter in a pan, then remove from the heat and blend in the flour. Return to a gentle heat and cook for a minute, stirring. Remove the pan again and add the milk a little at a time, stirring well so that no lumps form. Return to the heat and bring to the boil stirring, until thick and smooth, and cook for a minute. Remove the pan from the heat and beat in the mustard, nutmeg and cheeses; when these are well blended, stir in the egg yolks one at a time.

Whisk the egg whites with a rotary or electric hand whisk just until peaks form and tip over when lifted on the whisk. Using a metal spoon, fold a tablespoon of the egg white into the sauce, then carefully fold in the remaining egg white working the mixture as little as possible so that air is not knocked out. Divide between the ramekin dishes and run a teaspoon around the edge of each dish. Bake in the oven for about 20 minutes or until well risen and golden brown. Serve at once.

Serves 6 to 8

Fresh Herb Pâté

If you have lemon thyme in the garden use it instead of common thyme. Add freshly crushed garlic if you like too. This pâté improves in flavour if you leave it to stand in the refrigerator for a while.

Preparation time about 5 minutes
Chilling time about 2 hours

6 oz (175 g) rich cream cheese
¼ pint (150 ml) double cream, lightly whipped
½ level teaspoon freshly chopped thyme
½ teaspoon freshly chopped dill
1 teaspoon freshly chopped chives
salt
freshly ground black pepper

Blend together the cheese and cream and stir in the herbs and seasoning. Turn into a ¾ pint (450 ml) dish. Cover and chill well before serving. Serve with toast or crisp biscuits.

Serves 4

Right: Vet's Midnight Snack, Black and Blue Open Sandwich and Crisp Bacon and Egg Open Sandwich (page 121).

Hereford Mousse

A quick and easy starter, but you really do need a blender or processor.

Preparation time about 5 minutes
Chilling time about 1 hour

1 small clove garlic, crushed
6 oz (175 g) cream cheese
15-oz (425-g) can consommé
1 tablespoon sherry
1 level teaspoon curry powder
a few snipped chives to garnish

Place all the ingredients except the chives in a blender or processor and purée until smooth.

Pour into 6 ramekins and leave in the refrigerator to set.

Just before serving sprinkle the top of each dish with the chives, and serve with finely sliced brown bread and butter.

Serves 6

Left: Antipasto (page 145), and Miranda's Herb Loaf (page 183).

Eggs Aurore

A colourful first course, good for summer meals.

Making time about 5 minutes

1 punnet mustard and cress
4 hard-boiled eggs
1 teaspoon lemon juice
¼ pint (150 ml) tomato mayonnaise (see page 178)
paprika

Cut and arrange the mustard and cress on 4 individual serving dishes. Cut the eggs in half lengthwise and place them cut side down on the cress.

Stir the lemon juice into the tomato mayonnaise and spoon over the eggs. Sprinkle with paprika and serve with thinly sliced brown bread and butter.

Serves 4

Stuffed Eggs

Serve with thinly sliced brown bread and butter for a first course, or double the recipe and serve with assorted salads for a main meal.

Making time about 10 minutes

4 hard-boiled eggs
4¹/₂-oz (120-g) can of sardines, drained
1 tablespoon lemon juice
1 tablespoon mayonnaise (see page 178)
salt and pepper
4 lettuce leaves
cayenne pepper

Cut the eggs in half lengthwise and carefully ease out the yolks into a small bowl. Drain the sardines, add to the bowl and mash very well with a fork. Add the lemon juice, mayonnaise and seasoning and mix thoroughly.

Spoon the filling back into the egg white halves, dividing the mixture equally. Place the lettuce leaves on four individual plates and put two stuffed eggs on each. Sprinkle with a little cayenne pepper.

Serves 4

Anchovy Stuffed Eggs

To 4 eggs, prepare as above and then stuff with a mixture of yolks, 2 teaspoons anchovy essence and 2 teaspoons of tomato mayonnaise *(see page 178)*. Taste and check before adding seasoning as probably all that is needed is a little pepper. Serve on a bed of lettuce.

Pâté Stuffed Eggs

To 4 eggs, prepare as above and then stuff with a mixture of yolks, 2 oz (50 g) smooth liver pâté, 1 tablespoon tomato or ordinary mayonnaise *(see page 178)* and salt and pepper depending on the seasoning in the pâté. Serve on a bed of lettuce.

Pitta Bread Egg Salad

Cold omelette isn't to everyone's taste, perhaps, but I think it goes extremely well with pitta bread and shredded salad. I first had it in Spain where they serve Spanish omelette cut in diamond shapes with drinks. Take these pitta bread salads, wrapped in cling film, with you on picnics.

Making time about 10 minutes

1 egg
1 teaspoon cold water
salt and pepper
knob of butter
1 pitta bread
butter
1 lettuce leaf, shredded
1 tomato, sliced
a few slices cucumber

To make the omelette, place the egg, water and seasoning in a bowl and beat lightly with a fork. Heat the omelette pan until hot, add the butter and when hot and frothy pour in the egg mixture. Using the fork, quickly draw the mixture from the sides of the pan to the centre to allow the uncooked egg to run underneath. Shake the pan and leave for a few seconds, draw from the heat, loosen the sides, fold in three and slip onto a plate. Leave to cool.

Split the pitta bread almost through lengthwise, and butter both sides. Lay a base of lettuce on one side and then slide the omelette in on top. Cover with slices of tomato and cucumber and fold over the pitta bread.

Serves 1

Chinese Omelette

You need a small 6 inch (15 cm) omelette pan if you want to make individual omelettes, otherwise make one large one and divide in half.

Preparation time about 5 to 6 minutes
Cooking time about 1 minute for each omelette

> *1 level tablespoon cornflour*
> *½ level teaspoon salt*
> *1 tablespoon sherry*
> *1 tablespoon soy sauce*
> *2 tablespoons corn or vegetable oil*
> *1 spring onion, chopped*
> *2 oz (50 g) button mushrooms, sliced*
> *9-oz (250-g) can beansprouts*
> *4 oz (100 g) peeled prawns*

Omelette
> *a knob of butter*
> *4 eggs, beaten*
> *2 teaspoons water*
> *salt and pepper*

First make the filling. Blend the cornflour and salt with the sherry and soy sauce until smooth. Heat the oil in a small saucepan and fry the onion and mushrooms for 2 minutes or until soft. Stir in the blended cornflour and cook the mixture over a low heat, stirring all the time, until it thickens. Thoroughly drain the beansprouts and stir into the pan with the prawns.

To make the single large omelette, heat the omelette pan and add the butter. Place the eggs, water and seasoning in a bowl and beat lightly with a fork. Pour into the pan and, using a fork, quickly draw the mixture from the sides of the pan to the centre to allow the uncooked egg to run underneath. Shake pan and leave for a few seconds. Place the filling into the centre, fold the omelette in half and turn onto a warm plate. Serve at once.

Serves 2

Egg and Mushroom Cocottes

These make a nice starter before a light main course such as fish. The quantities could also be doubled up for a meal for a vegetarian.

Preparation time about 10 minutes
Cooking time about 5 minutes

1 oz (25 g) butter
1 oz (25 g) flour
½ pint (300 ml) milk
4 oz (100 g) button mushrooms, thinly sliced
4 hard-boiled eggs
4.62-oz (131-g) packet instant mashed potato
good knob butter
salt and pepper
2 tablespoons top of the milk or single cream

Melt the butter in a saucepan, add the flour and cook for a minute. Blend in the milk and bring to the boil, stirring until thickened. Add the mushrooms, reduce the heat and cook gently for 2 to 3 minutes.

Cut the eggs in half lengthwise. Make up the instant mashed potato as directed on the packet, adding butter and some seasoning, and make a border around 4 individual ovenproof serving dishes. Place 2 egg halves in the centre of each.

Taste the sauce and check the seasoning, and then divide between the 4 dishes. Put under a moderate grill for about 5 minutes or until the sauce is hot through and bubbling, and the potato is brown. If the oven happens to be on you can of course heat the cocottes through in it.

Serves 4

Curried Egg Mayonnaise

Boil the eggs ahead of time if liked but spoon the sauce over just before serving.

Making time about 5 minutes

4 hard-boiled eggs
4 tablespoons mayonnaise (see page 178)
2 teaspoons lemon juice
½ to 1 level teaspoon curry powder, or to taste
1 tablespoon juice from mango chutney jar
salt and pepper
watercress

Cut the eggs lengthways in half and arrange on a serving dish or individual dishes.

Blend the mayonnaise, lemon juice, curry powder and mango chutney juice together and season to taste.

Spoon the mayonnaise over the eggs just before serving and garnish with small sprigs of watercress.

Serves 4 as a first course or 2 for a lunch or supper dish

Egg Mousse

This is an attractive and delicious first course.

Preparation time about 15 minutes
Chilling time about 1 hour

½ oz (1 packet) powdered gelatine
2 tablespoons cold water
10½-oz (298-g) can condensed consommé
6 hard-boiled eggs
¼ pint (150 ml) double cream
¼ pint (150 ml) mayonnaise (see page 178)
1 to 2 teaspoons curry powder
1 tablespoon mango chutney juice
salt and pepper
tomato, cucumber and watercress to garnish

Put the gelatine in a small bowl or cup, add the water and leave to stand for 2 to 3 minutes. Place the bowl in a pan of gently simmering water and stir until the gelatine has dissolved. Put the consommé in a measuring jug and stir in the gelatine.

Chop the eggs and whisk the cream until it forms soft peaks. Mix together the cream, mayonnaise, curry powder and mango chutney juice with the eggs and stir in three-quarters of the consommé. Taste and check seasoning and divide the mixture between 8 individual ramekins and leave to set.

Garnish each ramekin attractively with pieces of tomato, cucumber and watercress, and spoon over the remaining consommé. Chill well before serving.

Serves 8

Savoury Rice

A simple first course that can be quickly prepared for unexpected guests.

Making time about 20 minutes

> *4.37-oz (124-g) packet mild curry savoury rice*
> *4 oz (100 g) cooked peas*
> *4 hard-boiled eggs*

Cook the savoury rice as directed on the packet, for about 20 minutes, when all the water will be absorbed.

Stir in the peas and mix thoroughly, then divide the rice between four individual serving dishes. Cut the eggs in quarters and arrange 4 on each bed of rice. Serve at once.

Serves 4

SALADS

Most salads can be starters or main courses, and many can be used as a side salad to go with a pâté, mousse or soufflé. In the summer, a salad makes a nice alternative to a soup.

Salads are quick to make, more a matter of putting together than of preparing and cooking. The secret of success is variety. Use the freshest ingredients possible and combine them according to your own taste and imagination. Look for crispness and colour and a contrast of textures and flavours.

Be imaginative with vegetables from the garden and use tiny new potatoes, baby carrots and French or runner beans when they are plentiful in summer. Choose Spanish onions, which are milder than the English variety.

Salads should be put together just before serving, but mayonnaise or French dressing can be made in advance. You can buy very good mayonnaise too. Add flavourings of your own – curry powder, lemon juice, mustard, herbs.

Waistline Salad

All the ingredients are deliciously slimming foods. If making it for the family they may enjoy a cheese and chive dressing over the top *(see page 180)*.

Making time about 10 minutes

> *8 oz (225 g) cottage cheese*
> *4 spring onions, chopped*
> *a good pinch dried dill (optional)*
> *freshly ground black pepper*
> *4 oz (100 g) peeled prawns*
> *1 small green pepper, seeded and sliced into rings*
> *2 heads chicory*
> *1 lemon cut in 8 wedges*

Blend together the cottage cheese, spring onions, dill and black pepper. Coarsely chop most of the prawns and add to the cheese mixture.

Arrange green pepper rings and chicory leaves on 4 individual plates. Pile the cheese and prawn mixture on top and garnish with the remaining prawns. Serve with 2 lemon wedges on each plate.

Serves 4 as a first course or 2 as a salad

Prawn Salad

Prawns are a luxury but this recipe makes the most of them.

Making time about 10 minutes

3 eating apples, cored and chopped
juice of half a lemon
8 sticks celery, chopped
¼ pint (150 ml) mayonnaise (see page 178)
6 to 8 oz (175 to 200 g) peeled prawns
2 teaspoons tomato purée
1 lettuce, washed
1 lemon cut into 8 wedges

Mix together all the ingredients except the lettuce and lemon wedges.

Place a bed of lettuce on 4 plates and then divide the prawn mixture between them. Garnish each plate with 2 lemon wedges.

Serves 4

Rice and Prawn Salad

Only use fresh mint for this recipe. Mint is one of the herbs that does not dry well, and is the easiest one to grow in the garden.

Preparation time about 15 minutes

6 oz (175 g) long-grain rice
1 red pepper, seeded and diced
2 spring onions, finely sliced
4 oz (100 g) peeled prawns
1 level teaspoon paprika
1 level teaspoon dry mustard
½ level teaspoon salt
freshly ground black pepper
2 teaspoons caster sugar
1 tablespoon chopped fresh mint
2 tablespoons corn or vegetable oil
1 tablespoon white wine vinegar
juice of half an orange
a few drops of Tabasco sauce

Cook the rice in plenty of boiling salted water for about 12 minutes, until barely tender, or as directed on the packet. Drain well, rinse in warm water, and drain again.

Place the rice in a large bowl and stir in the red pepper, spring onions and prawns.

In another bowl blend together the paprika, mustard, salt, pepper, sugar, mint, oil, vinegar, orange juice and Tabasco. Add this to the rice mixture and stir very well until thoroughly mixed. Cover with a plate or piece of cling film and leave in a cool place for the flavours to blend.

Serves 4

Salad Niçoise

This salad needs careful and gentle tossing otherwise the egg and tuna will become too mixed in and lose their shape. *(Illustrated on the jacket.)*

Making time about 10 minutes

3 tomatoes, skinned, quartered and pipped
½ cucumber, peeled and diced
8 oz (225 g) French beans, cooked and cut in short lengths
1 small green pepper, quartered, seeded and thinly sliced
half a mild Spanish onion, finely chopped
about 5 tablespoons French dressing (see page 179)
1 cos lettuce cut in 2 inch (5 cm) slices
7-oz (200-g) can tuna fish, drained and flaked
2-oz (50-g) can anchovy fillets, drained
2 oz (50 g) small black olives
2 hard-boiled eggs
coarsely chopped parsley

Put the tomatoes, cucumber, beans, green pepper and onion in a large roomy bowl. Pour the French dressing over the vegetables and mix lightly.

Arrange the lettuce in the bottom of a salad bowl or serving dish, then spoon the vegetables over it. Arrange the tuna fish, anchovy fillets and black olives on top. Cut the hard-boiled eggs in halves lengthwise and place on the salad. Sprinkle with the parsley.

Serves 4

Tuna Mayonnaise

Serve this recipe with hot herb bread *(see page 183)*.

Making time about 10 minutes

  1 cos lettuce
  4 tablespoons mayonnaise (see page 178)
  2 teaspoons lemon juice
  $1/2$ level teaspoon mustard powder
  1 teaspoon finely chopped chives
  1 teaspoon tomato purée
  7-oz (198-g) can tuna fish, drained
  7-oz (198-g) can prawns, drained
  salt and pepper
  tomato wedges to garnish

Wash and dry the lettuce and arrange on a serving dish.

In a bowl, place the mayonnaise, lemon juice, mustard, chives and tomato purée, and mix thoroughly.

Flake the tuna fish and fold into the mayonnaise with most of the prawns until well mixed and coated. Taste and add salt and pepper if necessary. Pile on top of the lettuce and decorate with the remaining prawns and tomato wedges.

Serves 4 as a starter but would serve 2 to 3 as a light lunch or supper dish

Hors d'Oeuvres

For 3 or 4 people choose a selection of 3 or 4 ideas as listed below. Arrange on a large platter attractively in lines or, if the dish is round, in wedges.

Plain or curried egg mayonnaise *(see page 135)*
Artichoke hearts in French dressing *(see page 85)*
Mushrooms à la Grecque, served cold *(see page 90)*
Herrings with spiced cream and cucumber salad *(see page 72)*
Beetroot salad *(see page 157)*
Yogurt, mint and cucumber salad *(see page 160)*
Tomato and onion salad *(see page 162)*
Redslaw with horseradish dressing *(see page 166)*
Tomato and avocado salad *(see page 163)*
Avocado dressed salad *(see page 164)*
Sweetcorn and sour cream salad *(see page 173)*
Curried rice salad *(see page 176)*
Small pieces of smoked mackerel fillets or soused herrings
Tuna fish with finely sliced onion rings
Salami, either in slices or wrapped round cream cheese mixed with chives
Garlic sausage, thinly sliced, folded over and arranged attractively
Smoked hams in profusion – and try some raw hams too

Antipasto

Use a Spanish onion as they are milder than our English ones and are best for most salads. *(See picture facing page 129.)*

Making time about 10 minutes

3 large tomatoes, skinned
½ cucumber, thinly sliced
a few endive leaves, shredded
4 oz (100 g) Italian salami, sliced
2-oz (50-g) can anchovies, drained
7-oz (200-g) can tuna fish, drained
1 onion, very finely sliced into rings
small clove garlic, crushed
1 tablespoon chopped parsley
8 tablespoons French dressing (see page 179)

Cut each tomato into 8 wedges. Arrange tomatoes, cucumber, endive, salami and anchovies on 6 individual plates, finishing with a pile of flaked tuna fish and the onion rings on top.

Blend the garlic and parsley with the French dressing and sprinkle over the salads just before serving.

Serves 6

Beef Waldorf Salad

This salad is good served in winter when celery is at its best, and is a good way of making the last few slices of a roast joint go further. Jacket potatoes served with a large knob of butter make an ideal accompaniment.

Making time about 15 minutes

8 tablespoons mayonnaise (see page 178)
1 tablespoon lemon juice
4 red-skinned eating apples
4 sticks celery, sliced
2 oz (50 g) walnuts, roughly chopped
8 slices cold roast beef
watercress

Put the mayonnaise and lemon juice in a large bowl and stir until smooth and blended.

Quarter and core the apples. Cut 2 of those quarters into thin slices and leave on one side for garnish. Cut the remaining apple into dice, add to the mayonnaise with the celery and walnuts, and mix thoroughly.

Pile the salad onto a serving dish and arrange the slices of beef in rolls on top. Garnish with the apple slices and sprigs of watercress.

Serves 4

Ham Rolls with Bean Salad

When runner beans come in August, they are usually in abundance. Try them cold in a salad for a change.

Making time about 15 minutes

> 8 oz (225 g) runner beans, sliced
> a knob of butter
> 1 small onion, sliced
> 1 oz (25 g) almonds, blanched and shredded
> 2 oz (50 g) raisins
> 3 tablespoons French dressing (see page 179)
> 8 slices cooked ham

Cook the beans in boiling salted water for about 5 minutes or until barely tender, then drain well.

Melt the butter in a pan, add the onion and fry for about 5 minutes or until soft. Add the almonds and raisins to the pan and fry gently, stirring continuously, until the almonds are an even pale golden brown. Lift out the contents of the pan with a slotted spoon and drain on kitchen paper. Leave to cool and then stir into the beans.

Chill in the refrigerator until required and then toss in French dressing. Arrange the bean mixture on a serving dish and lay rolls of ham on top.

Serves 4

Summer Salad

I like to make this in summer when the potatoes are new and French beans can be picked straight from the garden. But it is equally good made in winter using old potatoes and a packet of cut green beans from the freezer.

Making time about 15 minutes

1 lb (450 g) potatoes, cooked
8 oz (225 g) French beans cut in 1 inch (2.5 cm) lengths, cooked
¼ pint (150 ml) mayonnaise (see page 178)
8 oz (225 g) tongue, cut in strips
lettuce
tomato wedges

Cut the potatoes into neat ½ inch (1.25 cm) dice and place in a large bowl with the beans and mayonnaise. Mix thoroughly.

Carefully fold in the strips of tongue, trying not to break them up too much.

Line a serving dish with a bed of lettuce, pile the salad in the centre, and garnish with wedges of tomato.

Serves 4

Italian Ham Salad with Crisp Croûtons

I keep croûtons in the freezer, as they are a bore to make just for one recipe. Fry a whole or half loaf when you have time on a wet day! They will keep in the freezer for 3 months, then when required just refresh in a hot oven for a few minutes *(see page 187)*.

Making time about 15 minutes

4 slices day-old white bread, crusts removed
2 oz (50 g) butter
1 clove garlic, crushed
8 oz (225 g) ham, cut in strips
4 oz (100 g) cooked peas
2 to 3 spring onions, sliced
3 to 4 tablespoons French dressing (see page 179)
lettuce

Cut the bread into ½ inch (1.25 cm) cubes. Melt the butter in a frying pan, add the garlic and stir lightly to mix. Add the bread cubes and fry until crisp and golden brown all over, and the butter has been absorbed. Leave to cool on a piece of kitchen paper.

Put the ham in a bowl with the peas and spring onions, and mix in the croûtons. When ready to serve toss lightly in French dressing.

Arrange a bed of lettuce on a serving dish and pile the ham mixture in the centre. Serve with new potatoes and a tomato salad.

Serves 4

Pineapple and Ham Gourmet Salad

An impressive first course, but would also make a delicious summer lunch-time salad. *(Illustrated on the jacket.)*

Making time about 10 minutes

1 pineapple
4 oz (100 g) lean ham, cubed
2 oz (50 g) raisins
3 to 4 heaped tablespoons mayonnaise (see page 178)
lettuce
cucumber twists

Cut the pineapple vertically into 6 wedges, and scoop out the flesh from each wedge in one piece. Cut off and discard the hard centre core then roughly chop the flesh and place in a large bowl. Keep the pineapple skins.

Add the ham, raisins and mayonnaise to the pineapple and mix thoroughly. Pile the mixture evenly back onto the pineapple skins. Place each wedge on a plate with a lettuce leaf, garnish with cucumber twists and serve at once.

Serves 6

Chicken and Pineapple Salad

Pineapple and chicken, a lovely combination, should be made into a salad when pineapples are at their best and cheapest.

Making time about 20 minutes

1 cooked chicken
1 small fresh pineapple
juice of 1 lemon
½ pint (300 ml) mayonnaise (see page 178)
salt
freshly ground black pepper
1 oz (25 g) walnuts
watercress to garnish

Remove the meat from the chicken. Slice the white meat carefully and then cut the dark meat into neat bite-sized pieces.

Cut the pineapple into slices horizontally, and remove the skin and centre core. Cut 3 slices in half and put on one side for garnish. Chop the remainder.

Blend the lemon juice with the mayonnaise and add a little salt and pepper.

Take 4 tablespoons of the mayonnaise and mix with the dark meat from the chicken. Place on a serving dish and then cover with the chopped pineapple. Arrange the slices of white meat on top and spoon over the remaining mayonnaise. Sprinkle with the walnuts and garnish the dish with watercress and the halved slices of pineapple.

Serves 6

Carnival Chicken Salad

A colourful chicken salad, perfect to serve in the garden on a hot summer day. Roasted chicken portions can be bought in many supermarkets.

Making time about 15 minutes

> *8 oz (225 g) long-grain rice*
> *4 to 5 tablespoons French dressing (see page 179)*
> *4 oz (100 g) garden peas, cooked*
> *15-oz (432-g) can pineapple pieces, drained*
> *8 oz (225 g) tomatoes, peeled, quartered and seeded*
> *6 cooked (roasted) chicken portions*

Cook the rice in fast boiling salted water for about 10 to 12 minutes or as directed on the packet, until just tender, and then rinse well in warm water. Drain thoroughly, turn into a large bowl and, while still warm, stir in the French dressing. Leave to cool.

Add the peas, pineapple and tomatoes to the rice and mix well. Taste and check seasoning and if necessary add a little more French dressing or seasoning.

Pile the rice onto a large serving dish and lay the cooked and cooled chicken portions on top.

Serves 6

Chicken Simla

This could either be served as a salad main course or a first course. If serving as a salad increase the quantity of chicken.

Making time about 10 minutes

  a good ¼ pint (150 ml) mayonnaise (see page 178)
  1 level teaspoon curry powder
  8 oz (225 g) cooked chicken, diced
  8 oz (225 g) seedless grapes
  1 red pepper, chopped
  lettuce

Place the mayonnaise and curry powder in a bowl and mix together. Stir in the chicken, grapes and red pepper, and mix thoroughly.

Arrange a bed of lettuce on a serving dish and spoon the salad into the centre.

Serves 4 to 6

Apple and Duck Salad

This uses the last cuts of a duck (or goose). If liked, you could use it for an open sandwich topping.

Making time about 10 minutes

1 eating apple, cored and sliced
1 tablespoon lemon juice
¼ pint (150 ml) soured cream
¼ pint (150 ml) sweetened apple purée (or a small can)
1 spring onion, chopped
8 oz (225 g) cooked duck meat, cut in neat pieces
salt and pepper
½ bunch watercress

Toss the apple slices in the lemon juice to prevent discoloration and then arrange around the edge of a serving dish. Retain the lemon juice.

Put the soured cream, apple purée, lemon juice from the apples, spring onion and duck in a bowl and mix together. Add seasoning to taste and then pile the mixture into the middle of the serving dish. Garnish around the edge with sprigs of watercress.

Serves 4

Sausage Splits with Minted Salad

This is an attractive way to serve sausages cold. Use large sausages as they are easier to fill. If you have no left-over cooked potato, cook potatoes in their skins until barely tender. While the sausages are cooking, plunge them in cold water and remove the skins, then continue.

Making time about 30 minutes

knob of dripping
1 lb (450 g) large sausages
1¼ lb (550 g) new potatoes, cooked
about 7 tablespoons mayonnaise (see page 178)
1 tablespoon chopped fresh mint
salt and pepper
2 hard-boiled eggs
lettuce

Melt the knob of dripping in a frying pan and fry the sausages gently, turning frequently until evenly brown (about 20 minutes). Lift out and leave to cool on kitchen paper.

Meanwhile cut the potatoes into ½ inch (1.25 cm) dice and put in a large bowl with about 6 tablespoons mayonnaise and the mint. Mix thoroughly, and add seasoning to taste.

Finely chop the eggs and mix with the remaining mayonnaise. Make a lengthways slit along each sausage and fill with the egg mixture.

Arrange a bed of lettuce on a round serving dish and pile the potato mint salad in the centre. Lean the sausages up on the mound of salad.

Serves 4

Sausage Medley

This is a nice, slightly different way to serve cold sausages.

Making time about 15 minutes

8 oz (225 g) long-grain rice
4 tablespoons French dressing (see page 179)
4 oz (100 g) garden peas, cooked
4 oz (100 g) sweetcorn, cooked
1/2 cucumber, diced
3 to 4 spring onions, chopped
1 lb (450 g) sausages, fried and cooled
salt and pepper

Cook the rice in plenty of fast boiling salted water for about 10 to 12 minutes, until tender, or as directed on the packet. Drain, rinse well, and while still warm turn into a large bowl with the French dressing and mix thoroughly. Add the peas, corn, cucumber and spring onions.

Cut the sausages at an angle in 1/4 inch (6 mm) slices, add to the bowl and mix thoroughly. Taste and check seasoning and leave in a cool place until required, for the flavours to blend. Pile into a dish before serving.

Serves 4

Beetroot Salad

Beetroot is nice if served this way for a change. Beetroot takes so long to cook that it is often easiest to buy it ready-cooked. Look out for piles of steaming beetroot in the greengrocer's, then you know that it is really fresh. Beware of slippery, slimy beetroot with the skin beginning to peel back.

Making time about 8 minutes

12 oz (350 g) cooked beetroot, peeled
3 to 4 spring onions, sliced
2 teaspoons caster sugar
1 teaspoon vinegar
1/4 pint (150 ml) natural yogurt
pinch cayenne pepper

Slice the beetroot very thinly and place in a shallow dish with the spring onions.

Blend the remaining ingredients together and pour over the beetroot.

Serves 4

Beetroot and Horseradish Salad

Expect this salad to be rosy pink, so serve it in a separate bowl from other salads.

Making time about 10 minutes

   1 to 1¼ lb (450 to 550 g) cooked beetroot, peeled
   3 tablespoons horseradish cream
   1 small eating apple, peeled, cored and diced

Dressing
   ½ level teaspoon salt
   ½ level teaspoon white pepper
   ½ level teaspoon caster sugar
   1 tablespoon corn or vegetable oil
   ½ tablespoon vinegar

Grate the beetroot coarsely into a bowl and stir in horseradish cream and apple.

Blend all the dressing ingredients together and then pour over the beetroot mixture and toss lightly. Taste and check for seasoning and then pile into a small serving dish.

Serves 4, with other salads

Chicory and Pepper Salad

An unusual salad that can also be served in individual dishes as a first course.

Making time about 10 minutes

1 lb (450 g) chicory
juice of one lemon
1 red pepper, seeded and diced
1 green pepper, seeded and diced
about ¼ pint (150 ml) mayonnaise (see page 178)

Cut the base from each head of chicory and separate the leaves. Toss in the lemon juice to prevent discoloration.

Mix the red and green pepper together. Drain the lemon juice from the chicory and add sufficient to the mayonnaise to make a coating consistency. Fold in half the diced peppers.

Arrange the chicory in a serving dish, spoon over the mayonnaise and then sprinkle with the remaining peppers.

Serves about 6

Yogurt, Mint and Cucumber Salad

This is a good salad to serve in summer with barbecued food, very good with kebabs and steaks.

Making time about 25 minutes

1 cucumber
salt
1 pint (600 ml) plain yogurt
4–5 rounded teaspoons fresh chopped mint
freshly ground black pepper

Cut the cucumber into small dice leaving the skin on. Put on a plate, sprinkle with a little salt, cover with another plate and leave to stand for 20 minutes. Drain off any liquid.

Put the yogurt in a bowl and stir in the cucumber, mint and freshly ground black pepper. Cover the bowl and chill before serving.

Taste and check seasoning and turn into a dish.

Serves 6

Cucumber and Dill Salad

This is a simple Danish salad that is nice with fish, particularly trout and salmon.

Making time about 5 minutes

1 cucumber
1 tablespoon corn or salad oil
2 tablespoons hot water
2 tablespoons wine vinegar
2 tablespoons caster sugar
½ level teaspoon salt
white pepper
chopped fresh dill (or ¼ teaspoon dried dill tips)

Peel the cucumber, cut into thin slices and lay in a serving dish.

Blend the oil, water, vinegar, sugar and seasoning together and pour over the cucumber.

Sprinkle with the dill and serve.

Serves 4 to 6

Tomato and Onion Salad

Always a popular salad, it is even better if you take the time to peel the tomatoes.

Making time about 10 minutes

1 lb (450 g) firm tomatoes
2 medium onions
4 tablespoons French dressing (see page 179)
chopped chives

Plunge the tomatoes into a pan of boiling water for about 10 seconds, then pour off the water and put in a bowl of cold water. The skins will then slip off very easily. Slice tomatoes across thinly.

Very thinly slice the onions and arrange with the tomatoes in layers in a serving dish, finishing with a layer of tomato.

Spoon the French dressing over the salad and leave in a cool place until required. Just before serving sprinkle with finely chopped chives.

Serves 6

Tomato and Avocado Salad

Make a main meal salad by adding sliced cold chicken and, if liked, a little chopped spring onion. If time is really short, you don't need to skin the tomatoes, as long as they are firm.

Making time about 10 minutes

1 large avocado pear
1 tablespoon lemon juice
1 lb (450 g) firm tomatoes, skinned and sliced
About 5 tablespoons French dressing (see page 179)

Half an hour before serving, peel the skin from the avocado pear, cut in half, and remove the stone. Cut the flesh in slices and sprinkle with lemon juice to prevent discoloration.

Arrange the tomato slices around the edge of a serving dish and pile the avocado in the centre. Chill in the refrigerator.

When required spoon over the dressing and serve.

Serves 4

Avocado Dressed Salad

You can make the dressing in advance, but only make the salad at the last moment. It goes well with cold pork or ham.

Making time about 15 minutes

Dressing
  1 large avocado, skin and stone removed
  4 tablespoons corn or vegetable oil
  1 level teaspoon caster sugar
  ½ teaspoon French mustard
  2 tablespoons lemon juice
  ½ level teaspoon salt
  a good pinch black pepper
  a little green colouring

Salad
  12 oz (350 g) Cox's apples, peeled and diced
  1 small head celery, sliced
  1 bunch watercress, finely chopped
  1 oz (25 g) salted cashew nuts, chopped
  1 lettuce
  1 tablespoon chopped parsley

Purée all the dressing ingredients in a processor or blender.

Put the apples, celery, watercress and nuts in a bowl and pour over the dressing. Toss well.

Arrange the lettuce leaves around the edge of a large oval platter and pile the salad in the centre. Scatter over the parsley and serve with warm French bread and butter.

Serves 4

Coleslaw

This is a fairly classic recipe, and I often add chopped celery or diced apple if I have some to hand.

Making time about 10 minutes

1 small, hard, white cabbage weighing about 1½ lb (675 g)
¼ pint (150 ml) French dressing (see page 179)
salt and pepper
1 level teaspoon Dijon mustard
1 small onion, very finely chopped
2 carrots
5 to 6 tablespoons mayonnaise

Cut the cabbage into quarters, trim away any hard stalk, then finely slice into strips. Put in a large roomy bowl with the French dressing, seasoning, mustard and onion, and toss very well. Cover with a piece of cling film and leave in the refrigerator overnight.

Next day, grate the carrots coarsely and stir into the cabbage with the mayonnaise. If time allows, leave to stand for an hour in the refrigerator before tasting and checking the seasoning. Then pile into a large serving dish.

Serves 8

Redslaw with Horseradish Dressing

This is a good salad to serve with cold meat, especially roast beef.

Making time about 10 minutes

8 oz (225 g) red cabbage
¼ pint (150 ml) soured cream
1 to 2 teaspoons horseradish cream
½ clove garlic, crushed
salt
freshly ground black pepper
2 teaspoons vinegar
1 tablespoon finely chopped parsley

Shred the cabbage very finely, and place in a bowl.

Mix all the other ingredients together thoroughly, then pour over the cabbage and toss lightly. Chill in the refrigerator before serving.

Serves 4

Cabbage and Blue Cheese Salad

Danish Blue is a good cheese to use, but if you have any left-over Stilton that is even better.

Making time about 10 minutes

12 oz (350 g) hard white cabbage
1/2 teaspoon salt
1 teaspoon sugar
1/2 small onion, finely chopped
1 clove garlic, crushed
2 tablespoons corn or vegetable oil
1/2 tablespoon white wine vinegar
2 oz (50 g) Danish Blue cheese
1/4 pint (150 ml) soured cream
1 small eating apple, peeled, cored and diced
freshly ground black pepper
a little extra Danish Blue cheese to garnish

Cut the hard stalk out of the cabbage and then finely slice into strips.

Put the salt, sugar, onion, garlic, oil and vinegar in a large bowl and whisk together until blended. Then stir in the cabbage.

In another small bowl mash the cheese with a fork and stir in the soured cream. Pour into the bowl of cabbage, add the apple, and mix all together thoroughly. Taste and check seasoning, adding plenty of freshly ground black pepper. Pile into a serving dish and crumble the remaining cheese on top.

Serves 4 with other salads

Celeriac Salad

Blanching the celeriac first means that it keeps its colour and doesn't go brown. Take care not to cook longer than a couple of minutes, otherwise it will lose its crispness. This salad makes a good starter.

Making time about 15 minutes

8 oz (225 g) celeriac, peeled
juice of half a lemon
¼ pint (150 ml) mayonnaise (see page 178)
1 level teaspoon made mustard
3 hard-boiled eggs, sliced
4½-oz (125-g) can sardines, drained
1 tablespoon chopped parsley

Cut the celeriac into thin slices and then cut each slice into fine matchsticks. Put in a saucepan with the lemon juice and 1 pint (600 ml) water. Bring quickly to the boil and simmer for 2 minutes. Drain and rinse with cold water.

Put the mayonnaise and mustard in a bowl, mix together, then stir in the celeriac. Divide the mixture between 6 individual plates and garnish with slices of egg, the sardines and parsley.

Serves 6

Celeriac and Watercress Salad

Toss this salad just before serving otherwise the watercress goes limp.

Making time about 10 minutes

8 oz (225 g) celeriac, thickly peeled
juice of 1 lemon
1 bunch watercress
2 level tablespoons mayonnaise (see page 178)
salt and pepper

Cut the celeriac into match-like sticks, cover with water in a saucepan, and bring to the boil. Simmer for 2 minutes, then drain thoroughly. Put in a bowl with the lemon juice and leave to marinate for an hour, or longer if time permits.

Reserve a few sprigs of watercress for garnish and then chop the remainder. When ready to serve toss the celeriac, lemon juice, chopped watercress and mayonnaise together, and add seasoning to taste.

Pile into a serving dish and garnish with the remaining watercress.

Serves 4

Chicory and Endive Salad

A light crunchy salad that goes well with a fairly fatty cold meat such as pork or ham.

Making time about 15 minutes

2 small heads chicory
1 small endive
1 eating apple, peeled, cored and sliced
juice of half a lemon
4 sticks celery, chopped
1 oz (25 g) walnuts, chopped
8 tablespoons French dressing (see page 179)
salt and pepper

Cut the chicory into ½ inch (1.25 cm) slices and soak in iced water with the endive for 10 minutes.

Put the apple and lemon juice in a large bowl and toss so that the apple is well coated to prevent browning.

Drain the chicory and endive very thoroughly, and pat off any surplus water with kitchen paper. Add to the apple in the bowl, along with the remaining ingredients, and toss lightly into a large salad bowl and serve.

Serves 4

Potato, Apple and Celery Salad

Wash the potatoes and boil in their skins until just tender. Drain, cool, and peel off the skins. This helps the potatoes keep their shape and texture.

Making time about 10 minutes

1 lb (450 g) cooked potatoes
3 tablespoons French dressing (see page 179)
1 red-skinned eating apple, cored and cubed
5 sticks celery, sliced
salt
freshly ground black pepper
5 to 6 tablespoons mayonnaise (see page 178)

Cut the potatoes into ½ inch (1.25 cm) dice, and place in a bowl with the French dressing. Toss thoroughly while they are still warm. This will give the potatoes a delicious flavour.

Stir in the apple and celery and seasoning, cover with a plate or piece of cling film, and chill well.

When ready to serve, stir in the mayonnaise, taste and check seasoning and pile into a serving dish.

Serves 4

Quick Potato, Celery and Dill Pickle Salad

Buy dill pickled gherkins on the delicatessen counter. They go well with all cold fish salads, especially herrings.

Making time about 10 minutes

1 lb (450 g) cooked potatoes (or use a large can of potatoes, drained)
1 small head of celery, chopped
1 large dill pickled gherkin, sliced
¼ pint (150 ml) mayonnaise (see page 178)
salt and pepper
1 tablespoon chopped chives

Slice the potatoes and put into a large roomy bowl with the celery and gherkin. Add the mayonnaise with seasoning and mix all together very well.

Pile the mixture into a serving dish and sprinkle with chives. If time permits chill for a little while before serving.

Serves 4 with other salads

Sweetcorn and Sour Cream Salad

You can use frozen sweetcorn that has been cooked for a few minutes and then drained and cooled. Or if you like peppers, use a can of sweetcorn with added red and green peppers.

Making time about 5 minutes

12-oz (350-g) can sweetcorn kernels, drained
2 to 3 spring onions, finely sliced
¼ pint (150 ml) soured cream
salt and pepper
a few slices of red or green pepper to garnish

Put the sweetcorn into a bowl with the onions and stir in the cream. Season to taste and then pile into a small serving dish and garnish with the slices of red or green pepper around the edge of the dish.

Serves 4 with other salads

French Bean and Vegetable Salad

This is a good way of using up cooked French beans, but ideally they should be only just cooked and have a little crispness to them.

Preparation time about 15 minutes
Chilling time about 1 hour

8 oz (225 g) fresh French beans
2 oz (50 g) button mushrooms, quartered
4 tomatoes, peeled, quartered and pipped
¼ cucumber, peeled and diced
about 4 tablespoons French dressing (see page 179)
salt
freshly ground black pepper

Cut the French beans into 1 inch (2.5 cm) lengths and cook in boiling salted water for 10 minutes or until just tender. Drain and rinse in cold water.

Meanwhile put the mushrooms, tomatoes and cucumber into a bowl, add the beans and French dressing and toss well. Season with extra salt and pepper if necessary.

Chill well before serving.

Serves 4

Spring Salad Bowl

This salad is nice if you add sliced frankfurters to it.

Making time about 10 minutes

Dressing
4 tablespoons corn or vegetable oil
2 tablespoons wine vinegar
3 level tablespoons mayonnaise (see page 178)
1 level tablespoon tomato purée
a good pinch chilli powder
1 teaspoon caster sugar
juice of half a lemon

Salad
1 small lettuce, broken in pieces
8 asparagus spears, cooked (optional)
1 small onion, chopped
2 oz (50 g) button mushrooms, sliced
2 oz (50 g) young spinach, broken into small pieces
¼ curly endive, shredded
4 radishes, sliced
3 hard-boiled eggs

Blend together thoroughly all the ingredients for the dressing.

Put the salad vegetables in a large roomy bowl and toss lightly to mix well. Add the dressing just before serving, cut the eggs in quarters lengthways and arrange on top of the salad.

Serves 6

Curried Rice Salad

This salad has a mild curry flavour and you can add a little more curry powder if you like it really spicy. It is an ideal salad to serve to vegetarians.

Preparation time about 20 minutes
Chilling time about 1 hour

8 oz (225 g) long-grain rice
7-oz (200-g) jar mayonnaise
½ to 1 level teaspoon curry powder
1 green pepper, seeded and diced
1 eating apple, cored and diced
2 oz (50 g) raisins
4 oz (100 g) cashew nuts
salt
freshly ground black pepper

Cook the rice in plenty of fast boiling salted water for about 12 minutes, until tender or as directed on the packet. Drain well, rinse in warm water, and then drain thoroughly.

Meanwhile empty the mayonnaise into a large bowl and stir in the curry powder until well blended. Add the green pepper, apple, raisins and cashew nuts. Stir in the rice, mix thoroughly, and add seasoning to taste. Cover with a piece of cling film and chill in the refrigerator, to let the flavours blend.

When ready to serve, taste and check seasoning and then pile into a serving dish and serve either on its own or as an accompaniment to cold ham or pork.

Serves 6 to 8

DRESSINGS AND GARNISHES

Garnishes and sauces can make the dish. They enhance even the best ingredients and turn the simplest meal into a banquet.

A good salad needs a good dressing. French dressing is quick to make in quantity and can be stored in the refrigerator until required. Variations include adding garlic, herbs, curry powder, chives and tomato to the basic ingredients. Mayonnaise, either bought or home-made, can also be flavoured with herbs, tomato or garlic. Add chopped gherkins, capers and parsley to it and you have a tartare sauce to serve with the best quality fish.

Savoury bread, rolls, cheese fingers and croûtons all go happily with soup, and so do more unusual garnishes such as onion rings and toasted nuts.

Quick Home-made Mayonnaise

This mayonnaise is very quick to make and is all done in a blender or processor.

Making time about 5 minutes

> *1 egg, at room temperature*
> *1 tablespoon wine vinegar*
> *½ teaspoon caster sugar*
> *½ teaspoon dry mustard*
> *½ teaspoon salt*
> *a good pinch white pepper*
> *about ½ pint (300 ml) corn or vegetable oil*

Place all the ingredients except the oil in the blender or processor. Switch to a low speed to blend. Now add the oil in a slow steady stream until the mixture is very thick and all the oil has been absorbed. If necessary to blend the last amount of oil, turn off the motor and mix in with a small spatula, then turn on the machine and run for a few seconds.

Taste and check seasoning. If too firm, or not tart enough, add a little extra vinegar.

Tomato Mayonnaise

Add about 2 level tablespoons tomato purée to the blender with the last amount of oil.

Aïoli

Aïoli is the classic French garlic mayonnaise. Add two (or more, if you like) crushed cloves of garlic to the blender with the ingredients.

Tartare Sauce

Add 1 rounded dessertspoon each chopped gherkins, capers and parsley to the mayonnaise when it has been removed from the blender.

French Dressing

Making time about 3 minutes

> *½ clove garlic, crushed*
> *½ teaspoon dry mustard*
> *½ teaspoon salt*
> *good pinch freshly ground black pepper*
> *1 teaspoon caster sugar*
> *¼ pint (150 ml) corn or salad oil*
> *4 to 6 tablespoons cider or white wine vinegar*

Blend the first 5 ingredients together in a bowl and then gradually mix in the oil with a whisk or spoon. Stir in the vinegar, taste and adjust seasoning if necessary.

Garlic Dressing

Add the juice of 1 clove of garlic, crushed *not* chopped.

Fresh Herb Dressing

Add 1 tablespoon of freshly chopped mixed herbs – parsley, tarragon and basil, but mostly parsley.

French Dressing with Tomato

Skin, seed and chop a tomato and add it to the dressing.

French Dressing with Chives or Spring Onions

Add 1 tablespoon finely chopped chives or spring onions to the dressing.

Curry Vinaigrette

Add ¼ teaspoon curry powder to the basic French Dressing.

Cheese and Chive Dressing

An unusual dressing that is good served with a cold spiced beef salad.

Making time about 5 minutes

1 oz (25 g) Danish blue cheese
¼ pint (150 ml) soured cream
1 tablespoon chopped chives
paprika

Put the cheese in a small bowl, break up with a fork and stir in the soured cream. Add the chives and a good shake of paprika. Put into a small dish and serve with salads.

Serves 4

Quick Cheese Bread Rolls

These are simple to make and are lovely served with soup or a hot first course like Garlic Mushrooms with Cream *(page 91)*.

Preparation time about 10 minutes
Rising time about 35 to 45 minutes
Cooking time about 10 to 15 minutes

10-oz (283-g) packet white bread mix
6 oz (175 g) well flavoured Cheddar cheese, grated
1/3 pint (200 ml) hand-hot water

Put the bread mix in a bowl with 5 oz (150 g) of the cheese, stir in the water, and mix to form a dough. Turn onto a lightly floured table and knead lightly for 5 minutes until smooth and elastic.

Divide into 8 equal pieces and shape into rolls. Place on a lightly greased baking sheet, put inside a large polythene bag and leave in a warm place until doubled in bulk, about 35 to 45 minutes.

While the bread is rising heat the oven to 450°F, 230°C, gas mark 8. Sprinkle the remaining cheese over the rolls and bake in the oven for 10 to 15 minutes or until well risen and golden brown. Leave to cool on a wire rack.

Makes 8 bread rolls

Garlic Rolls

You could also make garlic bread. Make the cuts as you would for the rolls in a French loaf and butter both sides of each cut. Press back in shape, wrap in foil and bake.

Preparation time about 10 minutes
Cooking time about 15 minutes

2 cloves garlic, crushed
a little salt
3 oz (75 g) butter
freshly ground black pepper
6 crisp white bread rolls

Heat the oven to 400°F, 200°C, gas mark 6. Put the garlic, salt, butter and black pepper in a small bowl and cream until soft and fully blended.

Make 2 cuts an inch (2.5 cm) apart through each roll to within ½ inch (1.25 cm) of the base. Spread with garlic butter, on each side of the cuts, and press back into shape.

Wrap the rolls in a large piece of foil, or individually if you prefer, and bake in the oven for about 15 minutes. Serve warm.

Serves 4

Miranda's Herb Loaf

Make this when fresh leafy herbs are plentiful, otherwise just use parsley and a little dried thyme. *(See picture facing page 129.)*

Preparation time about 10 minutes
Cooking time about 15 minutes

> *3 oz (75 g) butter*
> *grated rind and juice of 1 lemon*
> *1 small clove garlic, crushed*
> *salt*
> *freshly ground black pepper*
> *3 tablespoons chopped fresh herbs or 1½ tablespoons mixed dried*
> *   herbs*
> *1 French loaf*

Heat the oven to 400°F, 200°C, gas mark 6. Cream the butter with the lemon rind and juice in a small bowl until soft and fully blended, then beat in the garlic, seasoning and herbs.

Cut the French bread almost through to the base in 1 inch (2.5 cm) slices. Spread between the slices with herb butter and then press the loaf back into shape. Wrap in a large piece of foil and bake in the oven for about 15 minutes. Serve warm.

Serves 6 to 8

Cheese Straws

These are very good if served with soup, and make a nice change from bread or rolls.

Preparation time about 15 minutes
Cooking time about 8 to 10 minutes

8 oz (225 g) plain flour
salt and pepper
4 oz (100 g) butter
4 oz (100 g) well flavoured Cheddar cheese, grated
a little beaten egg

Heat the oven to 400°F, 200°C, gas mark 6. Lightly grease 2 or 3 large baking sheets.

Put the flour in a bowl with salt and pepper and add the butter cut in small pieces. Rub in with the fingertips until the mixture resembles fine breadcrumbs, then stir in the cheese. Add sufficient beaten egg to make a firm dough, turn out onto a floured surface and knead lightly until the mixture is smooth.

Roll out to approximately ¼ inch (6 mm) thickness and then cut the pastry into narrow strips, rings, circles or fancy shapes such as diamonds. Carefully lift onto the baking sheets and cook in the oven for 8 to 10 minutes or until a pale golden brown. Leave on the baking sheets for a minute or two and then lift onto a wire rack to finish cooling. Store in an air-tight tin.

Rolled Cheese Fingers

Delicious served with soup in winter. For a change try spreading the slices of bread with ketchup before sprinkling with grated cheese – children will love these.

Preparation time about 5 minutes
Cooking time about 5 or 15 minutes

> *6 thin slices white bread, without crusts, buttered*
> *2 oz (50 g) Cheddar cheese, finely grated*
> *1 to 2 oz (25 to 50 g) butter, melted*

Either heat the oven to 425°F, 220°C, gas mark 7, or heat the grill to hot.

Sprinkle the cheese on the buttered side of the bread and roll up firmly. Place on a baking tray with the join underneath and brush with melted butter. Bake in the hot oven for 15 minutes or until crisp and golden brown. If the oven is not on, pop under the grill for about 5 minutes, but keep an eye on the rolls and turn over during cooking until evenly browned and golden.

Makes 6 cheese fingers

Roll Abouts

These go very well with drinks or with soup. They must be served warm.

Preparation time about 10 minutes
Cooking time about 10 to 12 minutes

8-oz (227-g) packet frozen puff pastry, thawed
3 oz (75 g) strong Cheddar cheese, grated
2 teaspoons milk
a good pinch cayenne pepper
a little salt

Heat the oven to 425°F, 220°C, gas mark 7, and grease a large baking tray. Roll out the pastry to an oblong the thickness of a 10p piece and about 9 × 8 inches (22.5 × 20 cm).

Mix the cheese, milk, cayenne and salt together and then spread over the pastry to within ¼ inch (6 mm) of the edge. Brush the edges with milk and then roll up from the long side like a Swiss roll.

Cut into 20 slices and then place on the baking tray evenly spaced and bake in the oven for about 10 to 12 minutes or until pale golden brown and flaky.

Makes about 20 roll abouts

GARNISHES

Croûtons

Remove the crusts from day-old slices of white bread and cut into neat dice or fancy shapes. Be sure not to make them too big as several must fit into a soupspoon. The bread should be no thicker than ¼ inch (6 mm). Fry in shallow or deep fat until golden brown, lift out with a slotted spoon and drain on kitchen paper. Serve in a small bowl with soup.

Fried croûtons may be stored in the deep freeze in a polythene bag. Take from the freezer and place, still frozen, in a hot oven at about 400°F, 200°C, gas mark 6 for 5 minutes before serving.

Melba Toast

Toast thin slices of white bread, remove the crusts and then with a large sharp knife, split the bread through the middle. Then, either toast the uncooked side under the grill, or bake in the oven. If the bread is very stale, slice very thinly and place on a baking tray and put in a low oven until the bread is crisp and curls at the edges.

Onion Rings

These add extra flavour to soups. They can be simply fried in a little butter until golden brown and tender, or they may be coated in milk and flour and fried in deep fat until golden brown and crisp.

Toasted Nuts

Flaked almonds, pine nuts and spiked almonds can be lightly toasted under the grill until pale golden brown, or fried gently in butter until golden. They not only add flavour but add crunch to the salads and toppings. If you use peanuts, try the dry roasted variety.

Index